SCARED SiLLY

my goal is to
not be insecure
in life - in
relationships -
in my abilities -
but to know the
true Power of God
who lives in side
me — — and,
to act accordingly!

Janet
8-7-13

SCARED SiLLY

taking on your fears, worries, and what-ifs

MARCY BRYAN

Standard®
PUBLISHING
Bringing The Word to Life
Cincinnati, Ohio

Published by Standard Publishing, Cincinnati, Ohio
www.standardpub.com

Project editor: Lynn Lusby Pratt
Cover design and photography: Scott Ryan
Interior design: Dina Sorn at Ahaa! Design

ISBN 978-0-7847-2067-7

Library of Congress Cataloging-in-Publication Data

Bryan, Marcy, 1962-
  Scared silly : taking on your fears, worries, and what-ifs / Marcy Bryan.
     p. cm.
  Includes bibliographical references and index.
  ISBN 978-0-7847-2067-7 (perfect bound : alk. paper)
  1. Fear--Religious aspects--Christianity. I. Title.

BV4908.5.B79 2007
248.8'6--dc22   2007021280

13 12 11 10 09 08 07   9 8 7 6 5 4 3 2 1

To my daughter, Meghan,
who did the one human thing
that made this book really possible—
she fell off a horse.

ACKNOWLEDGMENTS

First and most obvious: God, who in his humor and kindness provided this assignment as yet another example of being a loving, mighty, and involved Father.

Second and also obvious: my husband, Kevin, and daughter, Meghan, who have had to put up with not only my painful fear and subsequent healing process but also the birthing of this little book. Thanks for loving me in spite!

Third and should be obvious: Dale Reeves, Lynn Pratt, and all the staff at Standard Publishing, who took my yammerings and made them way better. I couldn't have done it without you.

Fourth but not so obvious: Terry Lewis, who heard my story and said, "I think that would make a good book," and thus encouraged a publishing company to consider a new approach to a serious project.

Fifth and obvious only to me: Meghan Bryan who wrote colorful notes of encouragement, gave daily you-can-do-it hugs and back rubs, and made countless little trays of "brain food" consisting primarily of Diet Coke and decorated ice cream. Darling, there is no daughter quite like you.

Sixth and somewhat obtuse: Kevin Bryan, Scott and Jamie Shuler, Jana Sooter, and my mother, Gerrie Fleenor, who read all 65,369 words (give or take a few) and offered helpful comments and energizing enthusiasm that kept me going during crunch time.

Finally and perhaps the most obtuse: the many friends and family who said over the years, "You ought to write a book." To them I say, "There. Happy now?"

I have known a great many troubles,
but most of them never happened.
—MARK TWAIN

CONTENTS

INTRODUCTION

iT WAS AN ACCiDENT

Never say "Oops!" Always say "Ah, interesting!"
—Anonymous

There are probably thousands of reasons why fear imbeds itself into people's hearts: traumatic moments in childhood, years of unresolved anger and resentment, a monstrous lack of grace and forgiveness toward self and others, honest-to-goodness physical overload, a personality that's more stressed out than serene, a shredded self-esteem, and possibly the Pillsbury Doughboy. I started unraveling the roots of my own fears . . . uh . . . by accident.

My daughter Meghan had begun Western-style horseback-riding lessons as an extended therapy for a learning disability. Imagine a therapist discussing possible programs with a then ten-year-old: "You're having trouble reading, so how about horse-riding lessons?" Meghan: "Uh . . . cool!" Personality note: My daughter is not a bat-out-of-you-know-where kind of kid. She's more of a going-to-start-sorta-slow child. Cautious yet curious, that's my girl.

This whole riding-something-huger-than-you was fairly stressful, but in a good way. And the typical good-stress things happened: the horse shook his head, the horse bent down to eat grass, and the horse swished some flies off its rump.

Until one day. Through a freak set of circumstances, Megh fell off at almost a gallop and landed hard, rolling in the dirt. By the time we reached her, her face was covered in blood, and her forehead had a huge (OK, huge to *me*) gash just above her left eye. It took seven whole stitches to close it up. Megh survived the experience fine. And I had to be revived only twice, using the medically sound method of drinking large amounts of Diet Coke provided by the caring ER staff.

That night my sleepless, fretful, caffeine-soaked mind replayed the mishap incessantly and in nauseating detail, often with more deadly results. So it was no surprise that by morning I was, to use the technical term, a basket case. (Question: Where did that phrase come from? I think it should be *padded cell case* or *loony tune case* or *funny farm case* or something more etymologically appropriate.) I was a trauma mama, a wigged-out woman, *eek*ing and freaking . . . you get my drift.

Needing to pull myself together, I set out for a walk in the fresh autumn sunshine. Halfway through yet another poor-me prayer, a thought stopped me in my well-worn gym shoes.

You are living in the what-ifs, Marcy, it said. *Stop that.*

Perfect, I thought. *Wait until I tell my husband I'm on my way to my own little padded cell, for sure. OK, fine. I'm going wacko—so let's just hitch up the horses and go in style.*

Then I thought back a real reply: *What should I do about the what-ifs?*

Say the what-is, came the response.

The what-is?! I screamed—in my head (I wasn't quite bonkers yet). *What are you talking about? My daughter could have been killed!*

The thought continued, *What is the reality of this moment?*

OK. Grumble . . . grumble. The reality is that Meghan is fine. The horse had bucked to the side, in fact, to avoid her. Horses are smart like that. Besides the cut on her head and a dirt-burn down her face, there were no other injuries or trauma at all, puzzling even the doctors. Pause. *Somehow*, I reluctantly continued (careful to keep the conversation inside my head), *whether I saw it at the time, accept it now or not, God was and is still in charge. And whether I feel it or not, God loves Meghan . . . and he loves me.*

Tears of frustration scalded my cheeks. *Great! Now the neighbors will think I've lost my mind.*

Say it out loud, came another thought.

Grrrr.

Yet as I spit out the what-is phrases under my breath, through free-flowing tears and dripping nose, I realized that my whole world had revolved—for as long as I could remember—around the what-ifs. *What if I get sick when I travel?* (even though I rarely do). *What if I freak out on a plane?* (even though I never have). *What if my husband leaves me?* (even though there were days). *What if that weird pain is cancer? . . . What if I die—or worse? . . . What if something happens to Meghan? . . . What if I don't have any more children? . . . What if we lose everything?*

The what-ifs had sucked the very life out of me, leaving a shame-filled, self-hating corpse of a Christian. I was breathing, but it was only to allow me to exist. I had quit *living* years ago.

What a wonderful life I've had! I only wish I'd realized it sooner.

—Sidonie Gabrielle Collette

This book comes from the realization that the what-ifs have held absolute (or near-absolute) power over my life. In case there's a test at the end, here's the CliffsNotes version: The what-ifs are the vehicle through which fear enters the mind. As fear settles in, it can become a stronghold that cripples and destroys the soul. So identifying from whence the what-ifs come is the first step. Then we can practice ways to wake up to our putrid, lie-filled thought processes. After that, we replace those lies with the truths of God's reality and love—the what-is's—which I've decided are the opposite of the what-ifs: *What is the reality of the moment? . . . What is the truth about God and me? . . . What is the ultimate victory?* In this way, I can pinpoint the enemy's activity and his destructive plan, even in microscopic increments within my immediate circumstance.

It's that simple . . . and that complex. By using the Scriptures, tips, ideas, and exercises in this book, perhaps you or someone you love can be freed from the tyranny of fear, guilt, depression, and self-hatred. I'm not totally finished with the battle; perhaps I'll never be. But I have seen that in Jesus I am perfectly and completely loved, regardless of whether I'm brave or afraid, whole or sadly lacking. That faith makes freedom a possibility and joy more than a dishwashing liquid. It's the hope of Christ enmeshed in me, in the most wonderful way imaginable!

TAKE YOUR MEDS

Meditate on Isaiah 42:9:

"See, the former things have taken place, and new things I declare; before they spring into being I announce them to you." ◖◗

The notion of what-is quickly caught on with my family and friends—which means that the all-too-revealing and grammatically challenged question "What is the what-is of this?" now follows me everywhere. My husband reminds me of it almost daily (God bless him). My daughter brings it up when I'm stressed (isn't she precious?). My neighbor has begun to use it when I whine. *Sigh* . . . I've become my own object lesson.

☕ SOOTHING INTROSPECTION

Accidental Education

P. J. O'Rourke said, "Everybody in fifteenth-century Spain was wrong about where China was and as a result, Columbus discovered Caribbean vacations."[1] Have you ever discovered anything by accident? while getting lost looking for a place? while cooking? while making something?

Was it a good or bad discovery?

Why do you say that?

What famous "learning accidents" do you know of from history? (The invention of the telephone is one.)

How can you begin today to look at your mistakes as learning accidents, at least in front of your spouse and friends? ☕

In this book introduction, I'm supposed to sound inspiring and profound, so here goes: A journey is set before you—although you won't have to contend with airline delays, money exchanges, obnoxious foreign waiters, or weird languages. This journey is probably worse. Just kidding! At least you'll be able to stay near your own bathroom and drink *cold* Diet Coke or *hot* coffee. And we'll be venturing into something thicker and possibly denser than the thickest and densest jungle—our minds! (Humor-filled from the beginning, this book!) As a result of this journey, you may begin a change that is at the core of your being, one that will alter your thinking, your behavior, and your future. What a trip! Or at least you'll be thinking of others who should read this book and thus venture and be altered. How about *that* for a bargain?

> Strangely enough, this is the past that somebody in the future is longing to go back to.
>
> —ASHLEIGH BRILLIANT

I pray that you enjoy this book and that maybe you even read it more than once. I would love it if you laughed a lot and cried a time or two—laughter and tears are powerful healing tools. But most of all, I really want you to take the bits of truth you find, use any that are relevant, and realize that God is forever near (Psalm 119:151), surrounding you (Psalm 32:7), loving you (1 John 3:1), and healing you (Psalm 147:3)—whether you feel it or not.

SOOTHING INTROSPECTION

What's Your Goal?

What do you want to gain from this book?

Jot it down on an index card or inside the cover (if you dare).

If you're the one who's fearful:

Pray that God will help you discover the nuggets that will most help you.

If you're reading because of a friend:

Pray that your friend will feel God in a very real way as you love on him or her in Jesus' name.

The Dreaded Journal Activity

Buy a journal or three-ring binder or swipe one from your kids or local neighborhood children. Millions of dollars are wasted every year on three-ring notebooks and lined paper that school children supposedly need but never use. Be bold! You're reclaiming valuable resources like vinyl and wood pulp in the form of uncool school supplies.

There will be numerous opportunities to write down thoughts and feelings, make lists, and even create something. Keep track of your thoughts and insights in detail—they will come in handy if you end up on *Oprah* someday. Mae West once said, "Keep a diary, and some day it'll keep you." (My advice is to negotiate a book deal *before* going on the talk show.)

You can also write on sticky notes (one of my personal favorite journaling techniques of all time) and then stick them—in a sort of order—on the lined paper in the notebook. Don't forget to date the notes so you can make sense of them later when you need to reference a great thought for your book.

If you tend toward geekishness, feel free to make notes in your fancy-pants, high-tech PDA, which I do not have because my husband thinks I can't run one. That's not true, of course—just because I am unable to run an MP3 player without the aid of my twelve-year-old doesn't mean that I won't be able to run a PDA. OK, maybe it does mean that. But I ask you, gentle reader, shouldn't I be given the chance to *prove* my ineptitude? But I digress. Whatever suits you is great. Do the exercises whenever possible to get your money's worth out of all these words. And don't worry, I'll whine about this again.

These **P**otentially **H**elpful **Q**uestions are for further self-reflection or small-group discussion. The first three are at the end of each chapter, repeated again and again and again . . .

1. Grab your notebook and record one thought about this chapter, one positive thing that happened today, one Scripture that you like, and one way that God has blessed you.

2. What struck you as interesting or unusual in this chapter? Why?

3. Choose one Scripture that you will try to memorize. Write it down.

4. Have you ever gone horseback riding? Describe the experience.

5. What made you want to read this book?

BE AFRAID, BE VERY AFRAID

Fear is that little darkroom where negatives are developed.

—MICHAEL PRITCHARD

F ear—the hair-raising, bloodcurdling feeling that wakes you up at night or sends cold chills down your back on a hot day. It's the bullet time of emotions, making things feel surreal and exaggerated. Fear is the rush many seek through slasher films and death-defying roller coaster rides. It is now widely believed (*widely believed* here meaning "currently believed by myself and my mom") that these adrenaline-seeking individuals probably have some sort of deep emotional illness, whether they know it or not. (For the record, trying to make the family SUV spin around like a child's toy on a snow-covered parking lot consisting of a minefield of sequoia-size light poles on gigantic concrete bases is, according to this author, an indication of deep psychological issues and can cause undue stress in your passengers. So stop it. Thank you.)

Long, long ago, if you had been a Neanderthal, fear (according to certain "scientists") would have been a useful tool for you, because the world was a particularly scary and unsafe place—not unlike after-Thanksgiving sales today. Wild beasts wanted to eat you, as did wild plants. (Remember those giant pitcher plants in the 1974 television series *Land of the Lost*?) Existence depended on being strong, ready, and quick. Thus it was important to have an edge over the untamed and unfriendly elements—such as finding an abandoned cave to live in or climbing a tree with big leaves and branches to hide in or growing a lot of hair because Levi's jeans had not been invented.

Of course, according to certain "scientists," if you were a Neanderthal, you'd already be dead and probably worm food or in some display at the Natural History Museum of Boise.

STRESS FREE QUIZ

What Are You Afraid Of?

Billy Bob Thornton said, "I quit flying years ago. I don't want to die with tourists." Note as many of your fears as you can.

In the animal category: ___Snakes? ___Mice? ___Spiders? ___Other?

In the man-made category: ___Elevators? ___Bridges? ___Realtors? ___Other?

In the relationship category: ___Husband? ___Parent? ___Getting hurt again? ___Other?

In the religion category: ___Rejection? ___Going to Hell? ___Choir robes? ___Other?

In the life category: ___Failing? ___Being alone? ___Dying? ___Other?

In the miscellaneous category: ___Barry Manilow? ___Clowns? ___Dust bunnies? ___Other?

Health care professionals (previously known as doctors) tell us that fear is the body physically readying itself for danger. At the first sign of intense and imminent trouble, the body releases adrenal hormones, better known as adrenaline. This little chemical causes a plethora of activity. Proteins, fats, and carbohydrates are quickly processed, producing immediate energy for the body to use; muscles tense up; the heart beats more rapidly; and breathing becomes quick and shallow—all in preparation for instant action. Even the blood changes its makeup ever so slightly, allowing it to clot better.

Collectively, this is known as the famous fight-or-flight response, which certain "historians" believe was developed during Jurassic Park times. ("In ancient times they had no statistics, so they had to fall back on lies."—Stephen Leacock) It makes sense that these "historians" would say this because anyone born before, say, the Nixon administration felt the need to be ready to fight off enemies or take flight away from them. (And I suppose *fight-or-flight response* sounds better than *fight or run away screaming,* the latter being more accurate in many cases, including mine.)

> Of all the thirty-six alternatives, running away is best.
> —CHINESE PROVERB

But in today's society, we rarely have to worry about wild beasts or wild plants. We have other fears: terrorism, road rage, nosy neighbors, PTA meetings, male-pattern baldness, office parties, dust bunnies, and home businesses in the form of Tupperware, just to name a few. And although being strong, ready, quick, and possibly hairy might help you against these modern threats, they aren't the weapons they used to be.

IT WAS HOLLYWOOD'S FAULT

During the '70s, irresponsible Hollywood moviemakers coerced the people of earth into participating regularly in wanton fear. I, being a "people of earth," fell prey to such evil mind control. It was during that time I read, and then voluntarily went to see, *Jaws* (1975). Why I would want to see such a frightening movie after being scared silly by the book still confounds me. Like any capable journalistic professional, I plan to blame someone else for my poor choices—in this case my friend Teresa, who worked at the theater and could get me in free.

In any form, *Jaws* was terrifying. And although I lived in Nebraska at the time (which hadn't been oceanfront property since maybe forever), I knew that if I *did* go to the ocean, sharks were lurking, waiting just for *me*. There was also a nagging concern that these carnivorous, cold-blooded beasts might rent a Greyhound bus and (work with me here, it was the '70s) drive to the Midwest—perhaps for the purpose of dining out—and sneak into our local lake or my bathtub.

> Dah dum. Dah dum. Dah dum, dah dum, dahdumdahdumdahdum.
>
> —ONE OF THE MOST TERRIFYING TUNES EVER FOUND IN A MOVIE
>
> (*JAWS*, IN CASE YOU CAN'T READ MUSIC)

All of this terror because of a strategically shot metal puppet! In case you're wondering, according to people who keep track of these things, the possibility of becoming shark bait when actually *in the ocean*—which I can safely say is a worst-case scenario—is 1 chance in 11.5 million.[1]

That same decade I saw *Alien* (1979) with tough woman Sigourney Weaver. Except for the parts about being in space and having to battle a demon-possessed, violence-bent squid, I wanted to be Sigourney Weaver. I would stand like her and wear black tank tops so we might be mistaken for twins. There was a slight problem with this great strategy: I was not quite blonde, wore glasses, had braces, and was shaped like Sigourney Weaver *not* in the slightest.

Alien was indeed a fashion inspiration, but it gave me the heebie-jeebies. And even though I never planned to be in the space program or near any teleportation devices, à la *Star Trek*, the possibility of suddenly flinging myself on the Thanksgiving table, my stomach erupting while a previously unknown baby alien leaped out, sent a clear message: space (and possibly Thanksgiving) was unfriendly and should be avoided.

The Shining (1980), in which Jack Nicholson took his innocent family to a creepy hotel to spend the long, ominous winter alone (thinking he wouldn't go insane), was another terrifying movie that I personally read the book *and* saw. You knew, of course, that when Jack *swore* he wouldn't go crazy, he would in fact do so immediately, thus traumatizing his family and—more importantly for the filmmaker's bank accounts and the point of this book—me!

But the piece of celluloid that broke the fearful camel's back was the rather graphic *An American Werewolf in London* (1981), a movie about two handsome and innocent college kids who become hideous, ravenous, deadly creatures. A quarter of a century later, I still don't like venturing out on a dark night across the heath . . . with a full moon and low-lying sinister fog everywhere.

Jack: David, before we go in there I want you to know that—no matter what happens to us—it's your fault.
—FROM THE MOVIE *AN AMERICAN WEREWOLF IN LONDON*

What does any of this have to do with fighting fear? Well, a lot, because each of us has our own events that have built teeny fear buttons inside our little respective brains. These invisible triggers are directly tied to the larger fight-or-flight hormone. So when the trigger is set off—whether from a memory, a smell, a phrase, a song, or anything from the '60s—those chemicals are activated in the same manner they were in your supposed Fred-Flintstone-esque ancestors. Your body thinks you are about to be eaten by a ravenous saber-toothed tiger or freakishly large plant, and it responds accordingly.

Scary movies were particularly problematic for me because, although I felt extremely afraid, they were very popular. Same with roller coasters. Here are terrifying devices with obscenely long lines where people intentionally wait an hour or more for three minutes of mind-numbing, gut-wrenching "entertainment." (I've always had a sneaky suspicion that such "fun" rides were created by angry, and possibly demented, engineers determined to get back at the human race for making them draw rectangles and do math instead of going out on Friday nights.) Even so, the movies were packed, and lines for roller coasters kept growing. How could all these people be sick and wrong?

PLENTY to WORRY ABOUT

It is well documented that fear is a huge problem in America. The Anxiety Panic internet resource (whose acronym is tAPir and whose mascot is, poignantly, the tapir—a shy, Jimmy-Durante-snouted animal) says that an estimated thirty million Americans suffer from an "illness of the nervous system that is medically recognized as an 'anxiety disorder.'"[2] These thirty million are those who suffer badly enough to seek medical help. That's one-tenth of the current population of the US, or twice all the people who live in New York City, Los Angeles, and Chicago combined. Of course, these numbers are probably just the tip of the proverbial iceberg.

According to tAPir and other reliable resources, many more struggle with fear in some way and either don't get help or have found ways to cope. I have a relative who is afraid of flying; he drives instead. I know someone who doesn't like elevators, so she uses the stairs . . . "for exercise." Several of my girlfriends, desperately afraid of getting fat, dramatically restrict their diets, spend great portions of their days working out, and engage in such recreational activities as throwing up. A lady in my prayer group is afraid of being rejected, so she remains aloof and distant (calling this behavior "professional"), even with her own children.

SWEATLESS EXERCISE

Something Stressful to Do

Find out how your body reacts to stress—keeping in mind that Richard Carlson said, "Stress is nothing more than a socially acceptable form of mental illness."

Keep a pad of sticky notes nearby. When you feel stressed, write down what your body is experiencing. See if you can tell what the adrenaline is doing in your system and how long it lasts.

Also note when you feel good and relaxed. What does that scenario look like?

What makes you feel that you can't handle something? Be as specific as possible. Is it when "one more thing" has occurred? Is it when you say yes to too many events/duties/service projects? Is it when you don't feel in control? Is it when you are tired or don't exercise or when you take in too much sugar or caffeine?

OK, I've got to quit. This is stressing me out.

Certainly fear can be an effective tool. I don't want to gain weight, but unlike my friends, I'm not motivated enough not to eat the piece of chocolate cake that is lying seductively on the kitchen table and calling my name. Nor will I put on the proper attire and go jogging—an exercise which I suspect was one of the punishments forced on us through Eve.

Unfortunately, dread often wants to be more than a handy-dandy motivational aid. It might start as such but can quietly grow deep, wrapping its roots into your soul. My friends who are afraid of getting fat? When they are honest with themselves and others, they really are afraid that if they don't look "perfect," people (their husbands, their influential friends, or their parents) will not like them, and that is something they can't stand. My relative afraid of flying really feels vulnerable about dying, so he takes control of every element possible to avoid that fate for as long as he can.

> Speaking in front of a crowd is considered the number one fear of the average person. I found that amazing— number two was death! That means to the average person if you have to be at a funeral, you would rather be in the casket than doing the eulogy.
>
> —JERRY SEINFELD

Dr. Susan Jeffers, a very smart woman (especially when it comes to panic), describes three levels of fear in her book *Feel the Fear and Do It Anyway*.[3] The first consists of top-level fears, which include situations, experiences, and preferences. (*Top level* here means the first layer, like the cherry is the top level of a banana split.) Eventually (and usually much sooner than *that*), they become (or are already related to) deep-seated fears. And it is those deep horrors—of rejection, of death, of hurting, of (fill in the blank)—that affect every particle of our lives, including our relationship with others and with God. We'll deal with all of this more in depth soon. But now it's time for another quiz.

Scary Influences in Your Life

Dave Barry said, "If you asked me to name the three scariest threats facing the human race, I would give the same answer that most people would: nuclear war, global warming and [Microsoft] Windows."

What is the scariest movie you ever saw?

Why did you see it? Was it because of an insensitive or sadistic friend or relative?

How much of it do you still remember?

Have you ever forgiven the person who talked you into going to that movie?

What is scariest book you ever read? (The current US tax information guide does not count.)

How old were you when you read it?

Who gave it to you?

Did you pass it on to someone else? Why in the world did you do that?!

We automatically react to all fears physically, but what is there to fear anyway? Everything, of course! Just look around you! The world is a terrifying place! It's not just measly saber-tooths looking for lunch anymore! Just watch the news! And you can tell there's a lot to fear because I'm using so many exclamation points! Like this! This means it's *really* scary!!!

For the sake of solid, authoritative writing, I looked up the headlines on three major news sources: cnn.com, foxnews.com, and nationalenquirer.dum. No wait, the last one was usatoday.com. Five of the top stories reported on these reputable Web sites in one day included 1) the bird flu has moved into Europe and is eyeing America, suggesting that if you leave your home for any reason and interact with humans, chickens, or other fowl, your future looks bleak; 2) if you speak only English, your career future is pretty bleak; 3) the stock market will be collapsing any minute, so your financial future definitely looks bleak; 4) a new and more hideous virus is preparing to assault your computer, so your technological future looks bleak; and 5) *American Idol* beat the Olympics in the contest of Most Popular Television Viewing, so the future of mankind looks absolutely dismal, and possibly hopeless. We're not even going to mention that thirty people died in various tragic ways, including one young man who was shot by his neighbor for stepping on the "friendly" neighbor's lawn.

There's more, but I don't want to scare you silly. You can see from these excellent and insightful examples, there is plenty to fear and worry about. (We will, of course, discuss all of the adverse emotions later; they are interlinked with fear via some magic mental/emotional/physical cord.)

TAKE YOUR MEDS

Do you relate to Ashleigh Brilliant's words? "I try to take one day at a time, but sometimes several days attack at once." Proverbs 3:21-26 can help:

"Dear friend, guard Clear Thinking and Common Sense with your life; don't for a minute lose sight of them. They'll keep your soul alive and well, they'll keep you fit and attractive. You'll travel safely, you'll neither tire nor trip. You'll take afternoon naps without a worry, you'll enjoy a good night's sleep. No need to panic over alarms or surprises, or predictions that doomsday's just around the corner, because GOD will be right there with you; he'll keep you safe and sound" (The Message). ◖▶

Your body's fight-or-flight response was most useful to help keep you alive from *physical* threats when dinosaurs roamed the earth. Even now, it's great if you are being chased by school children during a fund-raiser or fending off a telephone salesperson. But for most of each day, such powerful physical reactions are not needed. We are, in fact, mostly physically safe.

In general, our fears are calamities of a different sort. They are what-if disasters. For instance, although plane travel is safer, statistically, than any other mode of transportation, we can be overwhelmed by the thought *What if the plane crashes?* A plane crash is indeed horrible when it happens, but it does so less often than is implied by unbiased news sources such as CNN, FoxNews, and the *National Enquirer* (motto: The most stunning waste of ink and trees since 1952). In 2005, as an example, nearly eleven million flights carrying 745 million people safely took off and successfully arrived at their destinations.[4] Out of the eleven million, there were thirty-two commercial airline accidents resulting in twenty-two deaths.[5] Therefore, your chances of being involved in an aircraft accident are about 1 in 11 million.

If we (with the help of such interesting Web sites as fearless-flight.com) compare this to driving, we find your chances of being killed in a car accident are 1 in 5,000.[6] In other words, you take a greater risk driving to the airport than flying to your destination. But do you hear about all of the successfully accomplished flights? No, because this doesn't shock and sell.

Saying it differently, our modern-day stresses cause old-time reactions, which actually hinder our ability to cope with these new types of threats. It's like putting old-fashioned leaded gas (if you could find any) into your cool new Jaguar. You'll get around for a while, but the car will sputter and choke and eventually die.

ADRENALINE RUN AMOK

According to medical experts, today's stresses seem to keep our fight-or-flight response amped up because the body feels it must stay ready to react. Having adrenaline constantly coursing through your body might seem like a good thing, but this is because you aren't a medical expert. I'm not either, but I read several passages in an extremely large medical book and asked some very educated "healing specialists" (again, doctors to you and me) who went to school for a long, stinking time. According to these authoritative sources, having this hormone coursing through your body and (this is the important thing) *not using it up* is bad. (See what eight years of training can do for you?)

Because we don't have an outlet for built-up adrenaline (and in fact, we are rarely aware of all those extra chemicals coursing around our bodies, thanks to our bloodstreams), it stockpiles quicker than the national debt. (Ooooh! Something else to worry about! Sorry.) The result: panicky feelings that can happen to anyone at any time—even (and perhaps especially) during times of seeming calm. These excess hormones can amount to a panic attack. According to Dr. James Balch in *Prescription for Nutritional Healing*, "A panic attack is basically the body's natural 'fight or flight' reaction occurring at the wrong time."[7]

These chemically charged emotions might show up as a one-time experience. They could arise from a stressful illness or specific event or be linked with distinct behaviors or attitudes. But—here's the wonderful part about your body and your mind—they don't have to. Overwhelming fear and stress can show up apparently out of the blue. (Great. More to worry about.)

Suddenly your heart revs up so that you have enough strength to beat "it" up or beat it out of there, but what is the *it* you are fighting or flighting? You might feel dizzy as your lungs secretly take in extra oxygen, gearing you up (unknown to your own self) to run. But run from what? You might feel sick as your body dumps extra chemicals into your stomach and intestines in order to jettison anything that might slow you down. But why, and where must you go at such speed? Even your mental processes change. You might feel that things have become surreal as your mind prepares to deal only with surviving the imminent danger. But what, specifically, is the vicious enemy that immediately threatens you?

Stephen King says, "We make up horrors to help us cope with the real ones." Note: Some people (like one member of my own family who probably needs vast quantities of medical assistance) actually *seek out* adrenaline-rushing states of being by doing such unsafe things as watching several M. Night Shyamalan movies in a row, riding the Tower of Terror at Disney World, and hanging out of helicopters on a film shoot—just to name a very few real-life examples. All of these things my husband has actually done, some on a regular basis. No big deal.

But he recently became concerned that I hadn't washed the lettuce before making a salad. (I am not kidding.) Now I ask you, gentle reader, what kind of fearless living is *that*? I say, if you're going to be a crazy man who enjoys staring death in the face, then the state of your salad greens should be just another little laugh in the direction of danger, a wink at the hand of fate, a Pillsbury poke at the jiggly tummy of uncertainty.

STRESS FREE QUIZ

Look at Your Friends

Do you know people who are risk takers?

What are some of the dangerous things in which they take part?

Do they have any unusual quirks? strange rituals? Describe or illustrate.

Do they stress over things that seem odd to you?

Don't you just want to slap them sometimes? If so, describe in great detail in an e-mail to me. I need some ideas for my own sweet little risk taker. But remember what Rita Mae Brown said: "The statistics on sanity are that one out of every four Americans is suffering from some form of mental illness. Think of your three best friends. If they're okay, then it's you."

Not counting my husband or the paid actors on the fake reality TV shows or others like them, people are generally (and increasingly) *not* enjoying the constant anxiousness that seems to pervade society. In fact, people seem to avoid feeling afraid, except in extremely controlled places like movie theaters or money-sucking amusement parks. There is a good reason for this: the thrill seekers are *dying*. Have you kept up with the news? Each week individuals participate in some crazy stunt—base-jumping off buildings or skydiving or poodle wrestling—and things go terribly, horribly wrong.

Not really. I actually noticed the huge difference after the terrorist attacks of 9/11. We were living in Houston. Even after things got back to normal, everyone was more jumpy, more tense, and their eyes revealed a new, deeper level of angst. Our nice, reasonably safe world had shattered. It would never be the same. You knew it. I knew it. Our adrenal glands knew it and kicked into overdrive.

> If everything seems to be going well, you have obviously overlooked something.
>
> —STEVEN WRIGHT

Of course we got on with life. There were meals to fix, jobs to do, and children to parent and thus annoy. People got back on planes, children went back to school, and folks went back to work. But our anxiety really hasn't gotten better. I've followed the reports. As a nation, our use of anti-anxiety drugs increased significantly after the terrorist attacks of 9/11. The number of people complaining of headaches, tiredness, and depression—all symptoms of excess fight-or-flight hormones being dumped into the bloodstream over a prolonged period of time—immediately spiked and eventually leveled off, but (as of this writing) has really never gone down.

SOOTHING INTROSPECTION
Think About This

Initially, how did you react to 9/11? What about after several days?

Would you consider yourself changed by the event and its aftermath? If so, how?

After 9/11 what were some of the changes that happened in the people you knew? How are they doing now? Have you asked them?

According to several scientists and other eggheads who like to divide things up into little categories, there are three basic levels of fear. Actually, we now refer to this type of fear as stress because, I suppose, we feel afraid so often that we need a word befitting a constant state of being—and because *stress* doesn't sound as wimpy as *fear*.

The first level (described a few pages ago) is situational because it revolves around (surprise!) situations. These situations would include things that happen and things that require action. For example, Dr. Jeffers says aging and accidents "happen." The 9/11 attacks would cause a "happening" fear. Going back to school (or getting knee surgery) is a situation that requires planning and forced action. And they are all stressful.

At any of these moments, a wide variety of what-ifs begin to show their icky little heads. *What if there's another attack? . . . What if I'm not accepted? . . . What if I don't wake up from* surgery—or they put the knee in backwards? . . . What if . . . ?

A second level of stress (aka fear), according to Jeffers and others, involves the ego. This includes internal fears like rejection, failure, or loneliness. Now the what-ifs are visible and active, potentially shouting mob-like and waving miniature banners to stir up other emotions that may be lounging around enjoying a cappuccino or latte.

The third and final level of fear—the one that ratchets everything (hormones, imagination, coping) into overdrive, including charging up our fight-or-flight response—is the thought *I can't handle it*!

Even Christians seem to suffer from fear and stress. I don't have any cold, hard statistics, but I have noticed that when other believers find out I've struggled with fear, many immediately want to know all about it and often claim to have suffered with something similar.

Because of the vast amounts of experience gained while enduring this "adventure" I'm calling *Scared Silly,* I've found and made up some terrific things that might help you or those you know beat fears, worries, and what-ifs. We'll get to those soon. But first we have to do a little more fear fact-finding.

TAKE YOUR MEDS

Read Psalm 139—specifically, all of it. But here are some excerpts:

"O Lord, you have searched me and you know me. . . . You have laid your hand upon me. Such knowledge is too wonderful for me. . . . Where can I flee from your presence? . . . Even the darkness will not be dark to you. . . . Search me, O God, and know my heart; test me and know my anxious thoughts. . . . Lead me in the way everlasting" (vv. 1, 5-7, 12, 23, 24). ▪

1. Grab your notebook and record one thought about this chapter, one positive thing that happened today, one Scripture that you like, and one way that God has blessed you.

2. What struck you as interesting or unusual in this chapter? Why?

3. Choose one Scripture that you will try to memorize. Write it down.

4. Describe a time when you've been afraid. How old were you?

5. Would you consider yourself someone who struggles with fear? Why, or why not?

6. Is there something you do in order to avoid doing something else (such as taking the stairs instead of the elevator, taking an out-of-the-way route so as to avoid a long bridge, going places with friends so as to avoid driving alone)? When did you start doing this?

FEAR'S BEST FRIENDS

> If you want to test your memory, try to recall what you
> were worrying about one year ago today.
> —E. JOSEPH COSSMAN

W hile we're dissecting fear as if it were a frog in junior-high science class, let's get right into the guts, dig around with sharp instruments, try to make our lab partner gag . . . No wait! Frog guts aren't gross enough to do that to anyone, especially not me, sitting next to the cutest boy in seventh grade. It wasn't me! That's all I'm saying.

Ahem.

The guts to which I'm referring are depression and/or guilt, which work together to make fear even more powerful. However, *depression and/or guilt* is bulky and tedious to type, making it boring for you, the sensitive and astute reader, so they shall henceforth be divided up.

DOWNRIGHT DEPRESSING

Charles Schulz said, "I have a new philosophy. I'm only going to dread one day at a time." The *American Heritage Dictionary* defines *depression* as "the condition of feeling sad or despondent."[1]

This definition, while official, isn't all that helpful when you are describing those who struggle with this malady. So I've collected some other words to fill out the rather anemic offering: apathetic, blah, bleck, blue, blue funk, blueser, bone-weary, brown, bummage, bummed, bummed out, dead on the inside, dejected, despairing, despondent, discouraged, down, down in the mouth, gloomy, glum, heavyhearted, hopeless, ill humored, in the pits-ish, lost one's groove (or as the real hipsters say, mojo), low, melancholy, morose, out of body, overwhelmed, sad, saturnine, sorrowful, weary, weepy, weighed down, and woe is me. Take that, *American Heritage Dictionary*!

Depression, like fear, is a natural response to certain external things: the loss of someone or something; physical exhaustion due to excess exertion over a period of time; changes in hormones (no extra comment needed); the closing of your local Starbucks . . . Feeling depressed at such occasions is normal. And it takes time for your body to go through the loss, exhaustion, or changes in body chemistry to then reset itself—or at least that's what I have started telling people when I'm in a bad mood.

> The depressing thing about tennis is that no matter how good I get, I'll never be as good as a wall.
>
> —MITCH HEDBERG

Fear and depression seem to go hand in hand like Laverne and Shirley, Mickey and Minnie, Batman and Robin. It makes sense. If you are afraid, all that fear-drenched adrenaline will eventually become overwhelming, and you'll become depressed. If you are depressed, it can feel like you will never get better, which can make you afraid. Being afraid that you might never get better can easily make you more depressed. And on and on, deeper and deeper. Interestingly, many drugs used for treating people who suffer from anxiety also work well for those suffering from depression.

SOOTHING INTROSPECTION

Ask Yourself

Ashleigh Brilliant confessed: "I'm not always depressed: only when I think and feel."

Have you ever felt depressed? (If you are breathing, your answer will be yes, even if it's followed by "just a little.") Try to describe when and why you have felt this way.

Was it because of an argument or breakup? when your team lost the championship? when your hamster died? Be as detailed as possible.

If you get depressed often, have you identified any causes and/or triggers?

What are some things you've done to ease the depression?

How are those remedies working?

Do you know what makes your depression worse? Is it lack of sleep? certain types of food?

Please note that depression can be caused by medical conditions, a lack of a certain chemical in the brain, or other serious factors. A person can be emotionally depressed for so long that the body is depleted of the vital elements needed to correct itself. Medicines are often required at this point. Dorothy Parker, criticizing a performance by actress Katharine Hepburn, quipped, "She runs the gamut of emotions from A to B." But seriously, if you've been depressed (or overly anxious) to the point that it's affecting the way you live, please see your health care professional (or, um . . . doctor) immediately. Tell him a friend sent you.

People can become depressed because they live in a state of constant stress (previously known as fear). We've seen that there's much about which to be fearful. But how does fear produce depression? Looking briefly at high-class news sources such as CNN, FoxNews, ESPN, and TWC, I found these "uplifting" stories: a man who killed his roommate over toilet paper; recent lab tests revealed fecal matter in the ice of a nationally known restaurant chain; and it doesn't matter if you eat right or exercise, heart disease is probably in your genes. Even if we stuck with just those three items from the news, there's enough fear lurking around to brew up a reasonable depression about our world, our families, and ourselves. But there are other things even more insidious.

Although I don't want to bum you out, I must discuss them anyway in order to be a responsible writer. Each day these killers of joy and hope lurk around our homes, lives, and minds—stalking us as it were, waiting to find the opportune moment to pounce. I'm talking, of course, about junk mail and e-mail spam.

Actually, I'm talking about the *little* fears and worries (or frets, if you are from the Cold War era and thus possibly older than dirt, like me). "Worrying," explained Glenn Turner, "is like a rocking chair, it gives you something to do, but it gets you nowhere." Worrying over little things on the order of what to eat to stay on your insanely restrictive diet or what to wear to Girls Night Out adds enough stress and depression to our lives to kill laboratory mice within minutes. Personally, I think the medical community should test this. (And if the medical community makes amazing findings, all I ask is to be thanked privately with a large monetary gift.)

An example: You wake up with a headache for the third day in a row. Is it the weather? You look outside. It seems nice enough, so maybe it's That Time of the Month. Calendar check. Nope. *Gasp*. What if it's something really bad—a tumor or . . . aliens? (This is a logical conclusion since you've been watching informative, quality television in the form of *House* or *The X-Files* reruns.)

Then your child wakes up with dark circles under his eyes, complaining of not feeling well (= instant, intense fear/stress). What could be wrong? (It certainly can't be due to the fact that he ate chocolate cake three times yesterday because it was your birthday and then went to bed late and read a scary book and hasn't had a veggie for nearly a week because . . . well, just *because*.) What if there's something really wrong with him?! All this stress (and probably more) was generated within five minutes of climbing out of bed. And we haven't even dealt with getting ready for work and school, locating lunch money, finding the overdue library books, hunting down something for breakfast, relocating the now *lost* lunch money . . .

> I highly recommend worrying. It is much more effective than dieting.
>
> —WILLIAM POWELL

Worries can sap our energy and eventually bring on depression, and more importantly, they are limitless. We can worry about any aspect of life: money (having too little or having too much—a problem *I'd* like to work on), marriage (or singleness), children (having them or not, how they are doing, where to put the next handprint picture), getting older, what to wear (either to a special event, to work, or to Target, as the case may be), what shade to color your hair next, and whether to buy the dark chocolate kisses instead of the milk chocolate ones. (Informed author's note: Go dark.)

In 1967 some experts at the University of Washington compiled a chart of the major causes of stress and then assigned point values—the higher the total points, the more likely a person was to develop an illness.[2] Some of these were obvious. In fact, the first five on the list were negative: Death of a spouse led the list with 100 points. Divorce followed with 73. However, number six was (surprise!—or maybe not) marriage worth 50 points, number eight was marital reconciliation or retirement worth 45 points each, and pregnancy was 40 points—all of which are potentially positive. A change in financial state (either way) was worth 38 points. Other positive stress factors included a change in work hours or conditions, a change in residence or schools (20 points each), or a vacation (13 points). Oddly, Christmas (12 points) was considered more stressful than minor violations of the law, whether you got caught or not (11 points).

Other experts have divided the stressors into the simple categories of change, loss, and uncertainty. These are easier to remember but don't have fun point values. Of course, loss (like the death of a loved one or missing out on an expected promotion) connotes a negative experience. But what about *good* loss, like the shedding of extra weight or removal of gallstones? Apparently even these carry a certain level of change, extra emotion, and thus stress. So any change, good or bad, can increase your stress level (often equally so) and thus your depression potential. Any uncertainty—whether a good one (starting a new job) or a bad one (leaving the old one)—is stressful.

(In case you haven't noticed in these couple of paragraphs, there is some overlapping as the stressors refuse to stay neatly in their three simple categories. I find that stressful.)

Both studies left off the stress level of parenting, which I have calculated through the scientific method of experience to be worth about a million points. This means that babies, immediately followed by teenagers, should come with an endless supply of parental anti-stress medicine *as well as* an instruction manual, or risk being returned for a full refund.

> Children seldom misquote you. In fact they usually repeat word for word what you shouldn't have said.
>
> —ANONYMOUS

And not surprisingly, fear about the change (*What if this is bad?*) or about the loss (*What if I can't handle it?*) or about the uncertainty (*What will happen to me?*) increases the emotion, adding to the feeling of overwhelmedness, possibly ushering in a lengthy, first-class depression and/or anxiety.

GUILT BY ASSOCIATION

Guilt is another close buddy of fear. Erma Bombeck defined it even better—"Guilt: the gift that keeps on giving." This little gift, often passed generously from parent to child, links many negative feelings together. Want to ruin a good day—a day when the sun is shining, birds are singing, your jeans fit, and a surprise check arrives in the mail? Just let guilt sneak in: *You should give that money to the poor,* you berate yourself as you grab your car keys, *and not go splurge on a super cappuccino frappuccino from Star-(hand-over-the-big)-bucks. You don't need the calories. Your pants fit only because you air-dried them stretched upon a Stretch o' Rack.* (Please don't write asking where to purchase one of these beauties. I made it up. If I could invent something like this, it would be on HSN pitched by Suzanne Somers.)

Or even worse, guilt can disguise its voice to sound like a parent: *Good! Now you can make another small dent in that sinfully huge Visa card account. You know, we scrimped and saved for everything we had.*

Guilt uses "harmless" little words and phrases like *should, ought, you need to,* and *you have to.* I (although I'm not the only inspired person to do so) call them the wouldacouldashouldas. See how often they plague your life: *You should have done your exercises.* Or, *You would go see your mom (or crazy Aunt Lolly) if you really cared.* Or, *You could lose weight (or get a date or write a book) if you really wanted to—you simply must not want it badly enough.*

Guilt saps your strength and eats away at your confidence. It makes people step on the brakes almost involuntarily when they pass an empty police car.

> I have never smuggled anything in my life. Why, then, do I feel an uneasy sense of guilt on approaching a customs barrier?
>
> —JOHN STEINBECK

Clayton Tucker-Ladd, in his e-book *Psychological Self-Help,* says, "Guilt may cause depression." He also says, "Whoever makes us feel guilty is resented. In the case of guilt or regrets, you make yourself feel badly; thus, you become angry at yourself, and that anger is . . . the cause of depression."[3] I couldn't have said it better myself, especially since I don't have an impressive e-book. The Good Book says something similar: "My guilt has overwhelmed me like a burden too heavy to bear" (Psalm 38:4). This was King David's take concerning that icky little Bathsheba incident. But all types of guilt feel exactly the same—overwhelming, burdensome, and too heavy to bear.

Cathy Guisewite (of *Cathy* cartoon strip fame) said there are four major guilt groups: "food, love, career, and mothers." Generalized life guilt usually starts very young and is related to your primary caregivers (previously known as parents). These parental figures, especially if they are perfectionists, tend to put strenuous expectations on their progeny. If you currently are a parental-type figure and your house must be in real-estate-show-home-for-top-dollar condition (including bedrooms, play area, yard, and laundry room) but you're—this is key—*not trying to sell your home*, you may be a tad on the perfectionist side.

If your folks required you to have perfect attendance or straight A's at school or made you stay clean at all times—and gave you "the business" if you didn't do any or all of those things faultlessly—you might have grown up with a teensy bit of guilt bountifully bequeathed you by perfectionist parents.

> I don't know the key to success, but the key to failure is trying to please everybody.
>
> —BILL COSBY

If you tend to traumatize when things aren't just so or when something isn't done right (meaning only your way and to your liking) or you feel your image is tarnished by a disheveled husband or a "below par" performance by your child—you just might be a little bit of a perfectionist. OK, who am I kidding . . . you *are* one.

And though you're probably passing along many good traits to everyone, especially your children, you're also heaping on them some undue guilt. If you've had this done to you, then you know what a powerhouse this emotion can be. Long after the guilt giver is dead, his words ring in our ears: "You're going to wear *that*?" "When are you going to make something of yourself?" "You are just like your mother/father/other relative: stubborn, lazy, worthless, and (fill in the blank)."

Now just because *you* may have suffered at the hands of perfectionist guiltifiers who "invested" in your life, it doesn't mean everyone does. Take my family, for instance. We were the perfect example of well-adjusted, caring, self-starters. Even when we were teenagers, our rooms were never dirty, and our attitudes never needed adjusting. Yeah, right. I grew up in the '60s when guilt was the tried-and-true parental weapon. ("Eat your Brussels sprouts; people are starving in Africa." "Stop complaining. When I was your age, we had to walk to school in blinding snowstorms, uphill both ways, barefoot.")

However, during the anti-establishment '60s, we innocent children figured out (with the help of psychologists and other well-meaning ego-huggers) that we could use this same weapon masterfully against our parents. (The how-to was deftly portrayed by Hayley Mills in Disney's original *The Parent Trap* released in 1961.) My personal favorite guiltifying ploy was to claim (loudly and often) that I must be the adopted child because "my *real* mom wouldn't make me do . . ." My sister would walk around the house saying, "Cinderella! Cinderella!" as she did her chores. Yeah, we were fast learners.

> No matter how old a mother is she watches her middle-aged children for signs of improvement.
> —FLORIDA SCOTT MAXWELL

Guilt that aids and abets fear and depression is not your friend. Pray about the guilt in your life. Keep in mind, there's a useful kind of guilt. God highlights the bad things you've done (or the good things you were supposed to have done) to bring you to repentance—to change your direction, to draw you closer to him, to push you to depend on his strength more. The Bible says so (in 2 Corinthians 7:10; Romans 5:1-6; 1 Timothy 1:16; and Psalm 51).

But then God makes the guilt go away. Really. If guilt makes you feel overwhelmed, hopeless, and worthless to the point of despair, I'm guessin' you have a case of godless guilt instead of godly sorrow. The best way to know is by asking the Creator of all good things emotional to show you.

TAKE YOUR MEDS

John R. W. Stott said, "The Gospel is good news of mercy to the undeserving. The symbol of the religion of Jesus is the cross, not the scales."

Memorize 2 Corinthians 7:9-11 from *The Message:* "*Now I'm glad—not that you were upset, but that you were jarred into turning things around. You let the distress bring you to God, not drive you from him. The result was all gain, no loss. Distress that drives us to God does that. It turns us around. It gets us back in the way of salvation. We never regret that kind of pain. But those who let distress drive them away from God are full of regrets, end up on a deathbed of regrets. And now, isn't it wonderful all the ways in which this distress has goaded you closer to God? You're more alive, more concerned, more sensitive, more reverent, more human, more passionate, more responsible. Looked at from any angle, you've come out of this with purity of heart.*"

THE PERFECTIONISM TRAP

Perfectionism, when grown up, often appears as an all-or-nothing tendency. This is easily observed when someone proffers a compliment. The immediate response of a perfectionist (in his mind or out of his mouth) is, "Yeah, but . . ."

Graceless living is the sister of perfectionism and, like its sibling, depends on rules to survive—preferably for others to follow and itself to judge. It fancies measurable works instead of trusting another's heart. When an infraction happens, the love-lacking sisters of perfectionism and graceless living demand justice, swift and brutal.

> I got nothin' against mankind. It's people I can't stand.
>
> —Archie Bunker

A lack of grace (like perfectionism) is exhausting and joyless, imprisoning with the fear of failure everyone it touches. *What if I'm not doing it right?* Or, *How can I be sure I am saved? What if I'm not?* (I then hope any snotty, better-than-me Christians aren't either.) *But how do I* know? Or, *What if I die before I get it right?* News flash: We will; that is, die before we get it absolutely right.

These insane emotions demand a 100 percent guarantee of happiness (or satisfaction) in any given situation. *Anxiety, Phobias and Panic* describes this as "negative anticipation," which is "generated by a demand for a degree of certainty that is unattainable."[4] People want total assurance that what is feared won't happen. We civilized Westerners require that all foods, meds, transportation, and environments be completely and absolutely safe. This, according to the experts—and I feel they are pretty scientific (and biblical) about it, is impossible.

Perfectionism or a lack of grace often hides a fear of losing control. This what-if will send you down the trauma highway of mental illness faster than an endless game of Chutes and Ladders with a three-year-old on a rainy day. *What if I get sick while I'm away from home?* Or, *What if I go crazy on the plane and try to jump out?* Or, *What if I die?* Translation: *What if I lose control over life, myself, or my stomach? That would be horrible. I couldn't stand it.*

SWEATLESS EXERCISE

You Might Struggle with a Lack of Grace If . . .

- Keeping the rules is vital—even in a game of Go Fish with your three-year-old.
- You correct adults during activities and discussions.

- Getting something "right" will make you stay up all night—even though it's only your kid's Play-Doh show-and-tell project.
- You won't answer your door when your neighbor comes over to borrow a cup of sugar, because you haven't mopped the floor yet today.
- You use the words *should* and *must* in sentences with yourself or others more than two times a day.
- You want to fix what I wrote.

Make a list of wouldacouldashouldas you tend to hear in your mind. Do they come from your mom? your dad? your spouse? loony Uncle Clarence? a well-meaning Sunday school teacher? controlling friends? yourself?

Consider, as a first step, praying about these guilt-giving people. Ultimately, you'll need to forgive them and release the power their words (or their expertly performed guiltifying looks) have had in your life. But right now, just ask God to clarify some sources of the gift of guilt that has filled you to overflowing.

Who do *you* wouldacouldashoulda? Shana Martin understands the tendency: "I am not a perfectionist, I just have to make sure things are done right." 🔊

It's so interesting that Christians struggle with perfectionism. We know that the Scriptures repeatedly inform us that only Christ was perfect. Romans 3:23 says (all together now), "All have sinned and fall short of the glory of God." But we don't act like we really believe it, instead preferring the more impossible "Be perfect, therefore, as your heavenly Father is perfect" (Matthew 5:48).

Yet according to many scholars, the *be perfect* in that particular Scripture isn't a command that we are to accomplish. It's a character trait to aim toward, a beacon to home in on as we move through the muck of this life. It's like your three-year-old son getting up in the morning and telling you he's going to "shower and shave." You know that he can't literally shower and shave; he's going to splash around, play with his tub toys, and smear soap on his face. But you say, "Yes, it's time to shower and shave." He says it, you encourage it, and he accomplishes it to the best of his adorable toddler ability—trying to imitate what his daddy says and does. He just wants to be like his father.

And while someday the boy will indeed shower and shave in the manly sense of all men (unless he becomes that strange-looking guy from ZZ Top), we, though we should try to be like our Father, will never be able to achieve God-level perfection.

> The closest to perfection a person ever comes is when he fills out a job application form.
> —STANLEY J. RANDALL

Obviously you can't be perfect. If you could—if there were even the slightest possibility of your doing any of it flawlessly—then Jesus died for nothing. Scripture repeatedly says that he didn't, ergo you can't. Or you can't, ergo he didn't.

> If Barbie is so popular [*and thus perfect*], why do you have to buy her friends?
> —STEVEN WRIGHT

Hidden within perfectionism and gracelessness is fear. *If I do everything right, then they'll like me (or accept me or I'll be happy).* The hopeful "if" statement can easily morph into a traumatizing what-if question: *What if I do everything right and they still don't like me? Or, What if I can't do everything right? Will they like me anyway?*

These folks are often their own worst enemy. Their conclusions to any what-if (perhaps hidden even from themselves) are, *If I'm not perfect, I'm not acceptable* and *It doesn't count if I can't do it perfectly*—which come out sounding like "yeah, but . . ." in response to any compliment or achievement. Since no one can do "it" perfectly, most things in a perfectionist's life don't count. It is never enough.

C. S. Lewis said, "We are *all* fallen creatures and *all* very hard to live with."[5] When you expect yourself (or others) to perform to perfection, or penalize yourself (or others) because you (or they) have not acted faultlessly, you actually place yourself above God. You're saying, in effect, that you know better than the Creator of all things. Either that, or you don't need Jesus and what he did on the cross. Basically, you're insinuating that God and Jesus are wrong.

Forgive my boldness—mostly because I am often right there with you—but if you're going to dismiss Jesus' effort and pooh-pooh God's kindness, then you won't mind stepping over there, will you? I get nailed enough all by myself, thank you.

So . . . if we can't be perfect, why even try? Well, we shouldn't—especially not with the modern expectations of godlike flawlessness. We are in a lifelong process of becoming conformed to the likeness of Christ, learning to love as God loves, experiencing the wonderful intimacy of knowing and being fully known. These are impossible without Christ's death, God's help, and the Holy Spirit's living in us—and will be truly accomplished only after we go Home.

TAKE YOUR MEDS

Look at Hebrews 10:1-4, 11-14. According to this passage, what makes us perfect? What didn't (or doesn't) perfect us? In verse 12 it says, "When this priest had offered for all time one sacrifice for sins . . ." Who is the writer referring to? Verse 14 says, "By one sacrifice he has made perfect forever those who are being made holy." How can we already be perfect when we are not yet holy? What does that mean in our day-to-day lives? ◖▶

ANGER TURNED INWARD

"Anger always comes from frustrated expectations," said Elliott Larson. Anger and resentment are connected with fear in a variety of strange ways. Just look at some of the fears you have. We won't deal with *my* fears, because mine are all very sound and logical and, of course, have nothing to do with anger. DO YOU UNDERSTAND ME?!

Anger and fear are both reactions to a threat. Remember that good ol' fight-or-flight response? Well, you tend to fight better when you're (surprise!) furious. And you run away fastest when you are really scared. The body revs up to be ready for either.

If you are in a constant state where you feel threatened, like Nevada or New Jersey (just kidding!), you will potentially have both emotions swirling around looking for a way to save your skin. What will it be? Anger or fear? Fear or anger? Is the enemy smaller than you or threatening your loved ones? Rage rises up and you are ready for a fight. Is the enemy bigger than you or carrying weaponry, like a multilevel marketing kit? Run away! Run away! Generally, one of the two emotions will dominate in a person, at least in his reactionary behavior. However, where you find fear you'll definitely find a boatload of anger. And where there's anger, there's an ocean of fear.

Like fear, if the built-up anger is not released, seriously bad things can happen. Peter McWilliams said, "Guilt is anger directed at ourselves—at what we did or did not do. Resentment is anger directed at others—at what they did or did not do."

This isn't rocket science. If a kettle doesn't have any outlet for when the water boils, enough pressure will eventually build up to blow the lid off, causing expensive damage to your house. Same goes for your body. Nothing new here. Health care professionals were harping about this during the time of Aristotle, when they were still called doctors. Heart attacks, hypertension, and strokes can often be directly related to how we handle anger.

STRESS FREE QUIZ

How Do You Handle Irritations?

Elayne Boosler said, "When women are depressed, they eat or go shopping. Men invade another country. It's a whole different way of thinking." What do you do when you're irritated?

_____ Do you get angry? Are you Mt. Vesuvius ready to bury unsuspecting Pompeii?

_____ Do you become depressed? Are you a Gloomy Gus tossing your wet blanket onto anyone who ventures near you?

_____ Do you feel tired? Are you Weary Wanda barely making it through the day, looking like a zombie who needs a cappuccino IV?

_____ Do you feel overwhelmed and just want to escape to Aruba? the movies? your bed?

_____ Do you take control? Are you Sergeant Bilko on patrol?

_____ Do you become creative? Do you want to come up with clever names for every possible scenario?

Resentment is still anger but seems sneakier—it slips in when we self-righteously feel someone is not doing what he *should* do. (Ah, the wouldacouldashouldas arrive again!) Regardless of who should do what . . . when stuff doesn't go our way, we find ourselves angry and resentful. And we often respond as though someone should pay for making us feel this way—a cat must be kicked, as it were.

Unfortunately, if you are a "good Christian," you may have been taught that anger is a sin and thus bad; therefore, being a good Christian means never having or showing any negative emotions. This automatically puts you in line for stuffed-down, choked-back rage. And I'm sorry to say that this stuff doesn't go away by its lonesome. Worst case, it eventually erupts into Vesuvius-style violence: a seemingly mild-mannered preacher's wife blows a couple of golf-ball-size holes in her husband's back; a successful doctor flings his children and then himself off a fifteenth-floor balcony; a rifle-toting kid makes going to the mall a new type of target practice.

On a lesser level, people might blow their tops daily in more typical activities like withdrawing, yelling, cursing, and catapulting small furry animals across the room—resulting in loneliness, broken dishes, damaged relationships, and wounded pets. "I have a tremendous amount of anger," said Susan Sullivan, "but I like to save it for my loved ones."

If the tumultuous person doesn't strike outward, he or she might strike inward, manifesting in negative (and generally destructive) actions—like excessive eating, drinking, smoking, or shopping—that quickly become habitual or "holic." Inwardly turned anger might display an intense need to control, as exhibited by bulimia, sexual addiction, lingering depression, or a phobic fear. Yet the more a person tries to restrain uncontrollable things such as the environment or other people, the more overwhelmed he becomes. It's like trying to keep a dozen inflated beach balls underwater at once. The more one tries to keep everything in order, the more he fears that it won't be. Enter mental illness.

Anger isn't inherently bad—it can be healthy and helpful. "The world needs anger," said Bede Jarrett. "The world often continues to allow evil because it isn't angry enough." (By the way, have you noticed there aren't many funny quotations about anger? I resent that.) OK, anger *is* a part of living, so we might as well learn to release it in constructive, kind, and otherwise good ways. While we're at it, let's invest in the future of Christianity and the world and teach our children to do the same.

TAKE YOUR MEDS

Go to biblegateway.com and look up "God, anger." Read some or all of the passages. (There were fifty-nine when I did it.)

Was God ever angry? When? About what, and with whom? What did he do?

Do you know of any examples of Jesus' being angry? Look up keywords "Jesus, rebuked." Or you can check out Mark 11:14-17 and Matthew 21:12, 13.

What was the focus of Jesus' anger? What did he do?

What is one way you can aim to be like Jesus when you're angry? (Hint: It's not "clearing the temple" first thing.) ◑▶

Biblical anger is short-lived and has a bad memory. If just remembering certain events or people causes your blood pressure to rise and your face to flush or tears to well up in your eyes, then you can be reasonably sure you have some forgiving to do. Stop and ask God what and whom you need to forgive in that memory. Don't hold on to it any longer. More on that later. Just remember what Joan Lunden said: "Holding on to anger, resentment and hurt only gives you tense muscles, a headache and a sore jaw from clenching your teeth. Forgiveness gives you back the laughter and the lightness in your life."

STRESS FREE QUIZ

Whaddya Mean, Another Quiz?!

How often do you get angry on a good day?

____ I don't. They call me Sunshine at work, and I'm a delight at home.

____ Maybe once a day. And it's only a little.

____ Off and on. But it's justified.

____ Are you kidding me? Even on good days I'm ready for a fight.

__ WHAT DO YOU MEAN BY THAT CRACK?!

How often do you get angry on a bad day?

__ I don't. I told you they call me Sunshine, you chowderhead.

__ Maybe once a day. All day. But I try not to show it.

__ Off and on. But it's justified. And justice is swift because I carry a big stick.

__ Are you kidding? I can clear the room with a growl.

__ WHAT ARE YOU LOOKING AT? YOU WANT A PIECE OF ME?!

Brief but potentially helpful digression: Sometimes fear and anger arise when we feel we can't articulate our concerns, thoughts, opinions, preferences, or observations to another without being rejected or maligned. In these moments, trying to get a point across with regular words might seem impossible. It is then I find other methods of communication helpful; specifically, I print my message on a baseball bat. It's amazing how well Kevin "listens" when I'm "communicating" that way.

> Men and women belong to different species and communication between them is still in its infancy.
> —BILL COSBY

Actually, one of the most effective ways I've found to help people hear and understand what I'm saying is to use word pictures. The biblical term is *parables.* Jesus used these when he wanted to get a particularly difficult or abstract idea across to his disciples, who seemed to be, in general, slightly *dense,* a word that here means "just like me." I'm not above borrowing (read "stealing") inspiring ideas, so if it's good enough for Jesus, it's definitely good enough for me.

In *The Language of Love*, authors John Trent and Gary Smalley encourage you to formulate a fictional story (a parable) paralleling your thoughts and feelings in a way that is interesting and engaging to your designated audience.[6] Once your victim—I mean, your *audience*—identifies with what is happening in the story, you then unveil its true meaning. Nathan did that to David with great effect (2 Samuel 12), and Jesus did it throughout the Gospels (see Matthew 13 for a few examples).

Step 1. Think of your audience. Let's say I want to motivate my daughter to get her schoolwork done more quickly and without the usual guilt and trauma—because I want to finally win the Mother of the Year Award.

Step 2. Pick a broad subject with which your audience might identify. In this case it might be cooking, something Meghan likes to do as a hobby and is interested in doing as part of a career.

Step 3. Within the framework of that subject, form a story that describes how you are feeling. I might describe a head chef with a bunch of underling chefs, detailing as much as possible how a day might look in Head Chef Land. I'd then describe how a day might look if the assistant chefs took a long time to make the desserts, didn't seem to push themselves to get things done, or did their work sloppily.

Step 4. Describe how the head chef might feel. Better yet, I could ask Meghan how *she* thinks the head chef might feel.

Step 5. Make the connection that I feel the way the head chef feels.

Step 6. Rejoice in your communicative prowess.

Step 7. Tell it again the following week because kids lack a vital connecting link in their brains, which prevents them from remembering important life lessons—specifically, the ones their parents teach them. This occurs even though these same children can remember that you *promised* three months ago that they could have the new PS2 game as soon as it came out. Interestingly, they fail to remind you that they were supposed to keep their rooms clean and take out the trash as part of the acquisition deal. Hey, in a family, apparently it's every man for himself.

Anyway, this method of communication is so effective that *The Language of Love* was required reading in my classes on public speaking.

So fear, depression, guilt, resentment, perfectionism, unresolved anger, and all of those bad boys can form their own little negative train that can derail your life. Just knowing this is helpful. Knowing how to talk about these bad fellas is *really* helpful. Knowing how to beat them is *really, really* helpful. And that's what's coming in a chapter or two.

TAKE YOUR MEDS

Consider and memorize Isaiah 35:4:

"Say to those with fearful hearts, 'Be strong, do not fear; your God will come, he will come with vengeance; with divine retribution he will come to save you.'" ◖◗

1. Grab your notebook and record one thought about this chapter, one positive thing that happened today, one Scripture that you like, and one way that God has blessed you.

2. What struck you as interesting or unusual in this chapter? Why?

3. Choose one Scripture that you will try to memorize. Write it down.

4. Look up Matthew 11:28-30; 2 Corinthians 7:10; Romans 5:1-6; Psalm 51:10-17. What is the key thought in each verse? According to each passage, what does God do? What are we to do? What is the potential result?

5. Is there an area in your life that has to be "just so"? Why is that? Would you change this area? If so, how? Why?

6. Have you ever struggled with anger or depression? What was it like? How did you deal with it? If you still struggle, find a way to share that with a friend or small group so they can pray for you. Use Morse code if necessary.

For further help, there's a Resources section on page 247 of this book. Check it out.

BOO! DiD i SCARE YOU?

Television has brought back murder into the home—where it belongs.

—ALFRED HITCHCOCK

Fear and other negative emotions creep into our lives from a variety of places and in surprising ways, but none are stronger or more obvious than past experiences and memories. Your stinky little brother used to jump out and scare you every time you walked into a dark room. Your goofy uncle used to jump out and scare you when you came around the corner . . .

At about the age of twelve, after staying home from school with a fever, I went downstairs in the evening to do some homework. To get to our basement, one had to go into the garage and then down. As I worked on a typing lesson, the basement door in the adjoining room creaked slowly open and then slammed shut. I stopped typing and strained to listen.

"Hello?" I called out weakly. No answer. My imagination fired into hyperdrive as it mixed with bazillions of feverish brain cells. Within moments I was huddled under the typing desk, screaming hysterically. Frozen in complete and uncontrolled terror, I was sure I would die while my whole family blissfully made dinner, did homework, and watched TV eight feet above me. Mom finally heard the screams and raced downstairs to find her eldest daughter—a trembling wad of mucus and tears—starring in her own imaginary Alfred Hitchcock movie.

I found out that my dad had been the cause of the creaking door. He'd come down only to grab a bag of candy. By the time I started screaming, he was already back upstairs watching his John Wayne movie.

From then on I didn't really like being in suspense. And although that story is very funny to tell at dinner parties, I've just recently realized how much the experience and its resulting memory contributed toward developing my fear button. Beryl Bainbridge may have been right: "Everything else you grow out of, but you never recover from childhood."

SOOTHING INTROSPECTION

Do You Remember?

"Whenever I think of the past, it brings back so many memories," said Steven Wright. Think back to your childhood. What are some of your most frightening memories? Write them down. Pray that God will show you whether they have had any effect on how you handle fear and stress today.

You may not believe this, but when a person has an experience, chemicals are secreted and amassed in the brain.[1] All of the senses help in the production and collection of this data. Smell molecules are nabbed, analyzed to their teeniest makeup, and noted. Temperature is assessed and recorded. Taste and other physical responses have their own chemical patterns, all of which are duly gathered. This mass of subconscious sticky notes organizes into a kind of synthetic mob, which then cruises through the brain looking for a place to chill. Yo.

If the gang doesn't find any similar chemicals with which to join, it just blazes a path and makes a crib of its own somewhere in your mound of gray matter. If it does find other chemicals that are similar, they join to become an even larger biotic gang. As the mob trolls through the brain, a subtle trail is made, possibly hacked out with little molecular machetes or etched with a special brain drool.

This gang (having now named themselves the Blue Bloods, the Trauma Mamas, or maybe for the sake of simplicity, Fred) is easily located by other chemical sticky-note groups that follow the drool trails. Apparently, and I'm obviously guessing here, these emotional gangs make these paths because they're needy or lonely . . . or maybe they're just sloppy. But whatever the scientific reason, these poor chemicals just can't help it, so get off their little organic backs.

Throughout the process, the brain decides whether this mini emotional mob is good or bad; the actual experiences and chemical aftermath are often neither. It is the brain that makes them positive or negative by labeling each group. See how unfair and prejudiced your mind is? As more and more experiences are gathered, each is assessed, categorized, labeled, and grouped because the brain supposedly prefers neatness and order.

> You know, I think I could have the cure to AIDS or cancer in my head, but that brain cell is filled instead with old dialogue from the Brady Bunch.
>
> —MARY NEWTON

The neat-brain theory is probably true even of teenager brains that seem to thrive in filth and bedlam—if measured by their rooms, some of which haven't been cleaned since the arrival of the teens' first zits. If scientists *really* want to find a missing link, perhaps they should analyze the crud found growing in a young person's bedroom. I say this from personal experience.

Having once been a teenager—even though the idea totally creeps my daughter out—I often left ripe organic matter in the form of half-eaten bologna sandwiches or plates of spaghetti and glasses with two swallows' worth (a scientific measurement) of milk lying around until they (the crusted glop on the plates, or maybe the plates themselves) sprouted legs and walked. Of course, the primary reason any post-dinner matter would attempt movement would be to get away from the pile of dirty, hormone-oozing gym clothes shoved under the bed next to it.

> Cleanliness becomes more important when godliness is unlikely.
>
> —P. J. O'ROURKE

My daughter appears to be taking after her mother. The other day I found a wad of something under her bed that looked like the beginning of possibly three civilizations. Another day or two and we might have had to call Will Smith for *Men in Black III: The Louisville Connection*.

THE POWER OF MEMORY

Your brain decides whether one set of experiences is similar to another set or not. Take riding a roller coaster, for example. The sensation of falling while on the roller coaster has a similar chemical pattern of . . . well, *falling*. If you have ever experienced a very painful or unpleasant fall and its aftermath (such as, you got into trouble for getting your clothes dirty, you broke a limb in the form of your arm and felt sick, or you smashed your nose flat on the concrete and got blood all over your new outfit just before Uncle Bill's funeral), then the brain will try to file the sensations of the roller coaster ride in the same zone. Your body begins to associate roller coaster rides with the negative sensations of being out of control, getting hurt, feeling sick, and experiencing shame. Ergo roller coasters become bad.

How much and what type of emotion you felt during an experience also adds to how it is filed and thus remembered. Having a high emotional level during an event will make the memory stronger and last longer. That memory becomes a signpost, a billboard, a neon arrow pointing to other memories.

Weirdly (but not surprisingly), negative memories seem to outlast positive ones. My little trauma in the basement generated a huge amount of very intense fear. As a result, I remember it vividly. I can't, however, seem to recall much else from that time period, including the actual grade I was in or how many siblings I had.

Dave Barry, the award-winning humor columnist for the *Miami Herald,* wrote a book about the power of memory. He cleverly entitled it *Dave Barry's Book of Bad Songs,* and it is evil. Please do not *ever* read that book, because it will force many insidious tunes to be released into your brain, which are then ready to take over at the worst possible moment.

Being an irresponsible wife and mother, I made the mistake of reading this book aloud to my family during a long drive caused by a vacation. Ever since that time, my daughter will suddenly start singing in the middle of some serious math problems, for no apparent reason, "Muskrat Love." If she ends up on *American Idol*, I plan to blame Dave in my own popular, and possibly well-written, book.

> If you surveyed a hundred typical middle-aged Americans
> I bet you'd find that only two of them could tell you their
> blood types, but every last one of them would know the
> theme song from *The Beverly Hillbillies*.
>
> —DAVE BARRY

I repeat: do not read Dave's book! Simply know it vividly illustrates the mind's ability to retain information you once thought lost; and then it relentlessly and painfully bombards your conscious mind with this useless data, making Chinese water torture seem like a luxury spa treatment. Just try it yourself. Try for the next week *not* to sing "Don't Worry, Be Happy" as sung by Bobby McFerrin (or choose some other paltry, repetitive pop or country tune). You'll be begging for meds in no time.

SWEATLESS EXERCISE
Movie Memories

After viewing a movie or an event with others, ask them what scenes or elements they'll remember most. Also ask each person about his favorite scene and least favorite scene and why he judged them so.

See if you can figure out why each person identified with those particular moments.

Norbert Weiner—who has to be really smart because . . . well, just look at his name—wrote about humans and feedback. Barbara Frederickson and Marcial Losada—who are obviously really smart regardless of their not-so-nerdy names—studied Weiner's idea of feedback and found that it takes 2.9 positive feelings, experiences, expressions, or thoughts to fend off the languishing effects of one negative.[2] This explains why five minutes of CNN or an insulting remark or hearing the truly hideous song "MacArthur Park" (voted Worst Song Ever on popculturemadness.com) causes so much stress—your nervous system is being assaulted by negativity. (By the way, Meghan, "Muskrat Love" is number six on the list!)

Some memories are so hideous that we seem to block them out from our cognitive memory. A person who has suffered from sexual abuse might remember nothing about her childhood or that particular time period. However, she might have unusual behaviors that can't be explained but which ultimately help *prevent* recalling the emotion and the subsequent memory. She might not like the dark, for example, or become sick if she rides in the backseats of cars.

I read about a four-year-old boy who became unruly—yelling and screaming, totally freaking out—during lunches at preschool. His fits were so bad, several teachers had to carry him out of the room. The issue? He wouldn't eat his hot dog unless someone cut it up for him. Some of the teachers felt he was being demanding and needed to grow up. Sadly, further investigation revealed that the boy had been abused repeatedly by his father and his father's friends. Hot dogs couldn't stay in their original shape and remain part of his lunch, but the boy couldn't articulate why.

You may have had similar traumatic experiences. If so, certain fears and idiomatic behavior patterns could be a part of your daily life. I know this sounds simplistic, but if there has been abuse in your past, please find a kind, Christian counselor who can help you overcome the shame and horror you've been through. Please.

To recap: Fearful experiences can cause fear; traumatic experiences can cause fear even though we don't realize it; exciting experiences can be labeled as fearful by our over-organized brains; memories can be considered fearful because fear was the strongest emotion we felt at the time; and our memories are sorted and filed by the chemical makeup they produce, which means the memories can be considered fearful whether they are or not.

> The only normal people are the ones you don't know very well.
>
> —JOE ANCIS

Can you modify how your gray matter manages mental mementos? Yes, but we'll do that in another chapter so as to fool the brain. Right now it could be on the alert and ready to deflect helpful ideas. After all, it might be happy with its filing system and thus resistant to change. But after a few pages, we'll sneakily come back and fill the stubborn organ with possible ways to alter its patterns. We'll do this while it's thinking about those chocolate chip cookies in the pantry—I think they're made by elves. Can you picture them? Good, let your mind focus on them. 'Cause Barbara Jordan was right: "Think what a better world it would be if we all, the whole world, had cookies and milk about three o'clock every afternoon and then lay down on our blankets for a nap." Yummm . . .

TAKE YOUR MEDS

Meditate on Psalm 36:7:

"How priceless is your unfailing love! Both high and low among men find refuge in the shadow of your wings."

THE POWER OF PERSONALITY

The *Journal of Personality and Social Psychology* is a very scholarly magazine in that I hardly understood any of the words in it. Through intense study that required the use of an actual dictionary, I found several reports of federally funded, painfully complex studies about personalities, with titles like "Personality in Its Natural Habitat: Manifestations and Implicit Folk Theories of Personality in Daily Life." From what I can tell, the groundbreaking conclusion we can gather from this research is that our personalities affect the way we handle life and interact with others. Duh.

> You have a nice personality, but not for a human being.
> —HENNY YOUNGMAN

The idea that people have a unique blend of temperaments is as old as the hills. OK, it's as old as Aristotle, Plato, and Hippocrates. Modern psychology experts like Carl Jung, Isabelle Myers, Katharine Briggs, and John Trent took the classic ideals and divisions of personality (there were four) and further defined these traits, causing them to fall into several generalized continua: introvert or extrovert, thinking or feeling, a global view or detailed view of information, task oriented or experience oriented, creative or pragmatic, driven or compliant, and those who like *Survivor* reruns.

📺 SOOTHING INTROSPECTION

Who Are You?

How do you handle life? What makes you think as you do?

Are you an optimist? ___ Pessimist? ___ Ostrich/avoider? ___ Pretender? ___

How do you view life?

Do you see it as a game? ___ A battle? ___ A journey? ___ A pain? ___

Where did you first get this idea?

Was it from parents?___ Books? (List them if you can.)___ An experience? (Describe it.)___ A kind stranger?___ ☕

There are a ton of personality type indicators in the form of books and tests, which can be used to assess your individual blend of specific characteristics. PTIs are immensely helpful in understanding how you and those you love might react in various situations.

Please note: I don't believe that finding out what kind of bent you have predestines you to success or failure any more than I believe being left- or right-handed forecasts your success or failure (even though experts have made public statements that we left-handers are the only ones in our right minds). Nor does being one type of personality mean you will be that way throughout your livelong days. Not at all.

As a Christian, knowing that the Holy Spirit lives in me—and that he is a perfect blend of the best parts of all the personalities—allows me to be used by God more thoroughly. When I know my strengths and weaknesses, my bents and kinks, I can let God fill in the divots as needed or as I am conformed to be more like Jesus . . . whichever comes forth at the moment.

Submitting to God and his work in my life is not always a fun experience, but it is often surprising and always beneficial. And I become a more well-rounded person, spiritually speaking, as a result. (A plethora of "well-rounded" jokes is now coming to mind. But since my mother will read this, I must refrain from taking you down this humor path. Feel free to explore it yourself or with a few close, personal friends; and please inform me if you come up with some really good ones.)

Recent research like the aforementioned journal indicates that specific personalities can be more likely to struggle with fear or anger or depression. Again, because of the Holy Spirit, we are not doomed to stay this way, although it behooves us to be conscious of how we are bent and where we are lacking. Such understanding can also help determine a penchant toward überfear, thus giving us a heads-up and a leg up, as it were, on this problem maker. If you've never taken a PTI, it's worth doing. Though you may decide, as Jack Paar did, "I'm complicated, sentimental, lovable, honest, loyal, decent, generous, likable, and lonely. My personality is not split; it's shredded."

Famous People Who've Struggled with Anxiety[3]

Singers: Carly Simon, Aretha Franklin, Michael Jackson, Naomi Judd, Alanis Morissette, Barbra Streisand, David Bowie

Actors: Sir Laurence Olivier, Nicholas Cage, Johnny Depp, Burt Reynolds, James Garner

Actresses: Sissy Spacek, Sally Field, Kim Basinger, Olivia Hussey

Comics: Roseanne Barr, John Candy, Howie Mandel

Athletes: Earl Campbell, Jim Eisenreich, Pete Harnisch

Announcers: John Madden, Willard Scott

TV hosts: Oprah Winfrey, Susan Powter

Writers: Isaac Asimov, Anne Tyler, Charlotte Bronte

Artists: Charles Schulz, Edvard Munch

Others: Sigmund Freud, Abraham Lincoln, Charles Darwin, Sir Isaac Newton

Don't you feel special? ⚠

THE POWER OF IMAGINATION

Memories and personality types aren't the only doors through which the what-ifs can invade your mind. Having a great imagination is a huge plus when it comes to increasing fear. If you can quickly whip up a creative idea, movie concept, or pithy witticism, you also can easily produce a highly fanciful thought that can make you afraid. Panic disorder experts often describe people who struggle with fear as those who are sensitive, creative, imaginative types. That's why that list of famous folks who fear is full of artists and musicians.

You don't have to be artsy to be a candidate, however. If you have a creative side or deep-thinking side or musical side, then there is a chance you have the skill it takes to become fearful. Recall my basement boogeyman as just one example of how imagination feeds terror. Or take Steven Spielberg. I remember reading that he went to Hawaii to rest after making *Jaws,* but he wouldn't go into the water because he was sure the sharks knew what he had done and weren't too happy about it.

Evil people, like my husband Kevin, revel in messing with the minds of friends and loved ones by preying on their imaginations. One of Kevin's favorite things to do is to ask poignant, soul-searching questions, particularly in potentially stressful places such as airplanes. "Do you hear that noise? That engine doesn't sound right." Or out hiking, he'll say in a startled voice, "What's that? Did you hear that?" Or in everyday life as illustrated by this real-life transcript . . . Me (feeling stressed out): "Kevin, please tell me it'll be OK." Kevin (looking lovingly sincere): "Marcy, I promise you . . . we're all gonna die." Marcy (curling into the fetal position): "Aaaack. *Sob.*"

> After ten years in therapy, my psychologist told me something very touching, he said, "no hablo ingles."
> —DENNIS WOLFBERG

Obviously, your imagination can be assisted by your surroundings. Take the mall. Walk around its peppy, high-stylin' halls, and you'll wonder how you ever lived without *those* sandals or *that* beanbag couch or whatever else is being pimped there.

Mall visitation can cause deep feelings of immense dowdiness and social left-behindness. Fear is a natural reaction as you run for your financial life! Or if you are in a dark alley in downtown New York City with gobs of cash sticking out of every pocket, being afraid is not only to be expected, you'd be a fool to feel otherwise. Ditto for swimming in shark-infested waters, like within fifty miles of any ocean.

And there are other geographic locales that can assist the creative side of your brain and, thus, your level of trauma. Movie theaters (or living rooms) in which a scary or otherwise stressful movie is being shown are primary spots to brew negative thoughts. Forgive me if I'm belaboring the point. But if you watch something stressful, you are going to get stressed. That's their goal. Watching a horror movie, you *should* be horror-fied. Hence the name.

THE POWER OF THE MEDIA

Television and the Internet also feed people's fears. The American Academy of Pediatrics says that kids who watch just three or four hours of non-educational television a day will witness at least eight thousand murders before they leave grade school.[4] And that's just what they see on the news. Ha! I'm joking, of course—kids wouldn't watch the news even if it were the only thing on every channel.

Various mental-health Web sites, as well as famous psychologists (some of whom have written books), urge people of all ages to limit their intake of media in order to help control their thoughts and moods.

I'm starting a rumor right here that TV is the cause of all the problems in the world today, including my own personal weight gain and possibly male-pattern baldness (not that *I* have male-pattern baldness). Even so, we love our TV, don't we? It's a kind of best friend, even if it is a fickle type of friend that helps us watch countless people be murdered and witness various shades of porn for free (or for a low monthly fee). And according to Mary Anne Layden, co-director of the Sexual Trauma and Psychopathology Program at the University of Pennsylvania's Center for Cognitive Therapy, "Pornographic images stay in the brain forever."[5] So if this is true of all images, then in essence you have a huge library of pictures (moving and still) to pull from to accompany any topic. Pain and suffering thoughts? Here come images. Stressful thoughts? Here come images to match. Horrifying thoughts? Image order up! You get the picture . . . literally!

> [The] Supreme Court says pornography is anything without artistic merit that causes sexual thoughts. . . . No artistic merit, causes sexual thoughts. Hmm. . . . Sounds like . . . every commercial on television, doesn't it?
>
> —BILL HICKS

When we moved into our Kentucky house several years ago, cable wasn't available in our area (we live in the sticks); and we were too cheap to put in satellite. Before you get impressed, we have two TVs (not counting computers) and a homemade theater in our basement. So it's not like we're sitting in a tent, singing praises to our spirituality. You must know, I had satellite in Texas and loved it. I miss it more than anyone else in the family does. Especially during the Olympics. And the Super Bowl. And Christmas. And *Monday Night Football.* And Thanksgiving. And storms. And New Year's Eve. And when I'm bored.

Long story short (too late!), it's been more than two years and we still don't receive a single broadcast station (my TVs don't like external antennas). The downside: I don't know who won the last *American Idol* competition or whether *Lost* survived another season. On the upside: I don't avoid doing things (such as cooking and cleaning) like I used to. Who knows? I may even cave in and vacuum soon.

Someday we'll have cable or satellite again, I'm sure. But for now, the Grand Broadcastless TV Experiment continues. Send your donations c/o They Need to Rot Their Brains Too, Louisville, KY.

SWEATLESS EXERCISE

I Dare You!

Go on a total media fast for one week. OK, I'm *joking*! Go for one week without TV. Go twenty-four hours without your Internet, radio, and newspaper. Go half a day without your cell phone. Turn it off. Can you do it? Don't turn on any sounds—no DVDs, music, iPod, or anything.

Try it for a whole weekend.

Can you do it?

Can you stand the silence?

Replace the time you usually spend consuming media with something old-fashioned. Make a kite. Read a book aloud. (We've discovered *Peter and the Starcatchers* by Dave Barry and Ridley Pearson.) Make bread from scratch. Plant something. Sit outside and have a contest to see how many sounds you and your family can hear. Have a staring contest with a kid. Try to find all the constellations. Go to the library and check out a book.

The worst thing about media—TV, Internet, radio, podcasting, and the like—is that it not only pumps all manner of subtle stuff into our heads, it also prevents us from knowing how to live and enjoy silence. And times of silence are often when good, self-reflective, and thought-focusing activities like prayer, meditation, and Bible reading can take place.

If you haven't made it a practice to go TV-less, now's the time. Choose one night a week, shut the boob tube off, play games as a family, or (miracle of miracles) *talk!* Or don't talk. Read a book. Go for a walk. Do extra credit homework. Sit in silence. *Anything* is better. ●

THE POWER OF PEOPLE

Humans can also infuse us with fear and other negative things. For the benefit of my detailed and organized friends out there (you know who you are), let's classify these folks into five categories.

> Both men and women are fallible. The difference is, women know it.
>
> —ELEANOR BRON

I'm sure you've noticed how certain people tend to get you down, people who might be deemed difficult; they usually take the negative view of all things. For the sake of the upcoming clever illustration, they shall forevermore be called Negative Neds/Nellies.

Then you have your cynics—or "realists," or whatever spin-doctored name they call themselves—who see the glass as half empty and probably polluted because someone drank the top half and backwashed the rest. These shalt be the Cynical Sids/Sues.

Do you regularly interact with people you would call prickly? They seem consistently hard to please and generally in a bad mood. Often bosses, committee chairpersons, coworkers, or spouses are found in this category. Let's call them, just for fun, Cactus Jacks/Janes.

You may know a woe-is-me type of individual—let's call them Trauma Tims/Trinas. No matter what is happening in your life, their situation is always worse. And there is no way that you can get them—through trickery, bribery, or threat of violence—to think otherwise. "Oh," the woe-is-me friend says, "you have to have brain surgery? I should be so lucky. My head and neck have been throbbing for the past ten seconds. And my doctor, who is on my direct-line speed dial, says I just have to live with it until this afternoon when my masseuse can squeeze me in. I'm sure they'll have to take my *whole head* off and send it in for tests *immediately!*"

You may have Glen/Gilda the Guiltifier as a friend or relative. This person is endowed with a superpower consisting primarily of the amazing ability to persuade you to feel bad about anything good in your life (see chapter 2). Guiltifiers also use this superpower to make you do things that you wouldn't normally do—like escorting them to a raisin convention.

> We've been through so much together, and most of it was your fault.
>
> —ASHLEIGH BRILLIANT

It would seem easier to ship any or all of these folks off to a joyful little place like, say, Liberia, Siberia, or Iberia—because *beria,* as you might recall from geography class, is a Latin word meaning "this is a long, stinking way from anywhere." But we can't ship them off because, first of all, no one would be left—even happy-go-lucky folks aren't that way perpetually.

Second, the project would be prohibitively expensive—just imagine trying to check everyone's luggage.

The biggest and most important reason, however, is that negative people are *survivors* and would come back—even if you moved and left no forwarding address. Their experience would make them more difficult than before, as they counted and recounted their many trials ad nauseam (another Latin phrase, which means "making you want to eat that exploding candy and drink Diet Coke until your brain blows up").

STRESS|
FREE **QUIZ**

Difficult Persons

If we are honest with ourselves (especially me with myself), we can be all of these people—even in the time it takes to eat the hors d'oeuvres at a dinner party or make a simple phone call. It's an awful and humbling thing to consider, but because I'm a misery-loves-company kind of writer, let's do just that.

Who are the Negative Neds/Nellies or Cynical Sids/Sues in your life? (Be specific. Or at least use initials.)

In whose life are you the Ned/Nellie/Sid/Sue? (Be honest.)

Who are the Cactus Jacks/Janes in your life? (Write every name that comes to mind.)

To whom are you prickly? (List them all.)

Who are your Trauma Tims/Trinas?

In whose life do you trauma drama?

Who are the Glen/Gilda Guiltifiers, giving you the gift that keeps on giving?

In whose life do you guiltify? (If you have children, a spouse, parents, or siblings, consider putting all their names down—guilt tends to be a family affair.)

Since I'm still working on this just like you are, let's pray about these people in our lives, their influence on us, and our influence on them. I'm glad God has better and kinder ways than I do to deal with these types of people—including you and me when *we* are *they*.

TAKE YOUR MEDS

Meditate on Romans 12:1:

"Here's what I want you to do, God helping you: Take your everyday, ordinary life—your sleeping, eating, going-to-work, and walking-around

life—and place it before God as an offering. Embracing what God does for you is the best thing you can do for him" (The Message).

And while you're at it, ingest Romans 12:2:

"Do not conform any longer to the pattern of this world, but be transformed by the renewing of your mind. Then you will be able to test and approve what God's will is—his good, pleasing and perfect will." ◖▮

Be aware of who influences the way you think and feel. You may need to consider limiting your time with certain folks for a while—or at least until you buy earplugs and some relaxing tea.

To review: There are a number of things that can cause fear—your past, memories, experiences, personality, environment, friends, and even a great imagination. Take time to consider what impacts you on a daily basis. Some factors are easier to control than others. We will talk about that soon.

1. Grab your notebook and record one thought about this chapter, one positive thing that happened today, one Scripture that you like, and one way that God has blessed you.

2. What struck you as interesting or unusual in this chapter? Why?

3. Choose one Scripture that you will try to memorize. Write it down.

4. Make a list of the things that influence your thought processes. Be as specific as you can. Are you able to say that each element helps to lift you up? Which element is the best, and how? If there are negative elements, which is the worst offender? What can you do in the next few days to try to limit its hold on your thinking?

5. Review the "Difficult Persons" quiz on page 78. Which type of person affects you most? How? Which type do *you* most often become? Describe if you dare.

6. Extra credit challenge: Have a time of silence during this week. When might it be? How will you accomplish it?

Remember to check the Resources section on page 247.

BELiEViNG THE ENEMY'S LiES

I never know how much of what I say is true.

—BETTE MIDLER

Why are we who are *believers* afraid? What is there to fear really? The Bible has asked those same questions, as have philosophers and famous people throughout the ages. Why do Christians struggle with the what-ifs and all their terror—even though we know who's actually in charge, and we know about the glory that's coming?

I think fear has become such a huge struggle among Christians because we have believed the strategic lies whispered in our ears by our culture and the enemy of God. These falsehoods surround us daily, emanating through the airwaves and resonating in our heads. We even tell them to ourselves and then pass them on to our friends and our families because we can't seem to believe the truth.

> A lie gets halfway around the world before the truth has a chance to get its pants on.
>
> —WINSTON CHURCHILL

Before we identify these little falsities, let's define what a lie is so that you can achieve Thoroughly Informed Reader status, thus impressing your friends at parties. Looking up *lie* in the English dictionary is difficult, due to the fact that our English founding fathers required each word, by law, to have fourteen thousand different meanings. You'd be better off with a Spanish dictionary, or even a French, because each word has only two meanings. OK, they do tend to be direct opposites—but at least there's less to deal with.

However, we are English, so we must leaf through the millions of pages to get to the entry *lie*. Then we must sort through the bazillion definitions, all of which are almost, but not quite, exactly the same. My favorite online dictionary brought forth eleven entries in 1.2 nanoseconds, most of which fretted over the correct use of *lie* and *lay*. You *lay* something *on* something. (Ex: I will lay my head down on this table . . . *thunk*.) *Lie* is everything else . . . I think.

We would all agree that lies are bad because a *lie* is "a false statement or action, especially one made with intent to deceive" (my *Webster's New World Dictionary*, page 827). No Christian really wants to do that, even though we deceive on a daily basis.

Case in point: what weight is on your driver's license? Mine is a kind of guess—in this case meaning probably 10-ish pounds less than what is displayed on the scales of my health care provider. (I'm not sure how the earth's gravitational pull can vary so much from the geographic location of his scales to mine, but there it is. I don't make up the facts; I just abuse them.)

◧ SOOTHING INTROSPECTION

Enlightening Self-Examination

Lady Nancy Astor said, "I refuse to admit I'm more than fifty-two, even if that does make my sons illegitimate." When someone asks your age, how do you answer?

A. I pick a favorable number, which I report as my age, no matter how old I get or what evidence there is to the contrary.

B. I ask the asker, "How old do I look?" and enjoy watching him squirm as he tries to guess. If he is so rude to ask, he should feel my wrath.

C. I snap, "None of your beeswax!" and glare at the offending person before stomping off. It's uncouth to inquire about such delicate information.

D. I tell my real age and then say, "Thanks for bringing up such a painful subject," launching into a lifetime play-by-play until his brain melts from boredom.

E. I say I am ten years *older* than my real age. Then I enjoy the compliments of people who are amazed at how wonderful I look. ☕

Being an optimist, I prefer to label many of the lies I tell daily as *untruths,* which are defined by the *American Heritage Dictionary* as "being false." There appears to be a subtle but critical distinction between the two words: a lie is a deliberately deceitful act, whereas an untruth is simply not necessarily true. I identify with that. I don't intend to mislead the police with the less-than-accurate poundage listed on my DL; I actually intend to mislead *me.* That is a *huge* difference, pardon my pun. So although I can't think of an example at the moment, one could presume that an untruth clearly happens by accident, assuming the presuming is being made by altruistic and clueless aliens from other planets.

THE TRUTH ABOUT LIES

Why are such delineations important in dealing with the fear-filling what-ifs? Well, besides the fact that these delineations make me sound knowledgeable, we need to understand that all what-ifs are a combination of lies and truth. Even being afraid that (this is an official absurd-exaggeration alert) giant worm men of planet Xldhr might invade planet Earth, attack you and your family, take you back to their planet, and make y'all slaves . . . could be fed by a real fear—namely, having to be prepared for everything. How would you pack for such occasions? Should you take snacks? Do worm men resemble earthmen and thus need dental floss and luggage tags? Since we haven't traveled around the solar system, *could* there be worm people?

OK, maybe more terrifying on a non-inane basis are the clothing requirements of certain earthbound events—like what to wear to that fancy Christmas party. Or as it is here in Louisville, what hat to sport at the Kentucky Derby, our little two-minute horse race with more pre-event happenings than the Academy Awards and with almost as many bling-toting notables and their muscle-toting bodyguards.

If in each lie there is some truth, how do we tell which is which? *My daughter is sick. It could be serious, even life-threatening. Other kids have become sick and have died. I'm treating her cough and fever as a normal virus, but what if I'm wrong? The bird flu also causes a fever and a cough.* Or, *My husband might lose his job. What if he does? What if he can't find another one? We might have to sell the house. What if we end up on the street? Other families have had bad things happen, and they've ended up sleeping under bridges.*

> I was not lying. I said things that later on seemed to be untrue.
>
> —RICHARD NIXON

In any of these cases, except for the pathetic cosmic worm

example, there are bits of truth within the uncertainty of the what-ifs. And it's easy to let our minds sit in that mud pit because it seems a logical, normal place to be. If anything, we might label our what-ifs as slight overreactions, because we *know* that God ultimately and truly cares about us and loves us and will watch over us, right? *RIGHT?!*

TAKE YOUR MEDS

Grab your notebook and Bible. Through the Bible God speaks to you. ("Why is it when we talk to God we're praying, but when God talks to us, we're schizophrenic?"—Lily Tomlin.) Look for verses that indicate God's care of you as his child. When you find an especially uplifting verse, write it down. Try these for starters:

"I will lie down in peace and sleep, for you alone, O Lᴏʀᴅ, will keep me safe" (Psalm 4:8, NLT).

"I know the Lᴏʀᴅ is always with me. I will not be shaken, for he is right beside me" (Psalm 16:8, NLT).

"The steps of the godly are directed by the Lᴏʀᴅ. He delights in every detail of their lives" (Psalm 37:23, NLT). ▄▄

Unfortunately, in my life the untruths often rule. And though they seem innocuous and nonpoisonous, I believe they are the initial cause of much fear, pain, depression, self-loathing, and whatever other negative element I might harbor in my sweet—but human and thus depraved—little mind.

Ross Brodfuhrer, a gifted Bible teacher I know, once described in this general manner how lies affect us: Think of a glass of water as something totally pure. Let's say you know it's pure because it's in a clear bottle with the words *natural* and *spring* printed on its bluish label. Plus it cost nearly two bucks, so it has to be pure! How much strychnine will it take to make the water impure? According to chemical expert Ken Ownby—who knows a lot about this sort of thing and is a close personal friend—one molecule. OK, that's not *exactly* what he said. He used a bunch of impressively huge scientific words like *picograms/kg* and *botulinum toxin* and incomprehensible numbers like 3.9×10^{-22}, which just shows how smart he is.[1]

Ross's (and Ken's) point is, when *anything* is added to the pure water, either good or bad, it is no longer totally pure H_2O, meaning it becomes impure even if ever so slightly. You don't have to add enough strychnine to kill a person; one atom changes the integrity of the whole. (And in case you're wondering—it'll take more strychnine than that to do the job, although I can't tell you the exact amount because Ken won't let me.)

> Lady Nancy Astor: Winston, if you were my husband, I'd poison your tea.
>
> Winston Churchill: Nancy, if I were your husband, I'd drink it.

The pure/impure water illustration applies to truth and lies. How much falsity does it take for the truth to stop being pure truth? One atom's (or maybe I should say "one Adam's") worth.

The enemy doesn't have to make us swallow a big ol' corker; if he can get us to accept one little inexactitude, God's truth can be diluted, even just a teensy bit. Next comes another speck of untruth . . . and then another . . . moving us along from absolute truth toward total lie. Each drop of untruth takes us a step away from the real truth and makes it easier to believe more untruth the next time. Eventually (and unnoticeably) we end up neck deep in the muck and sludge of lies, wondering how in the world we got there.

THE ENEMY'S LIES

So what are the lies about?

God. God and you. God and his relationship with you. God and your understanding of his view of you. And although there are many variations of the lies (or untruths), they can be boiled down to just a few main ones.

1. God has certain standards, and you don't meet them. God is perfect, and therefore, he has some really tough requirements. All of the nasty, low-down things you've done in your past—and let's be honest, there are plenty—count against you, including the stuff from today. And . . . well, yesterday wasn't so hot either, was it, champ? God knows all of it. And I bet he's pretty peeved.

"Real" Christians shouldn't act or think like that and certainly don't talk like that, and they probably can tell what kind of loser you are; in fact, they might have told you so in no uncertain terms. Let's face it, you aren't really worthy of being loved—by God or anyone else.

2. There are consequences when God's perfect standards aren't met. God is just, and therefore, payment for any mistakes or mishaps must be made. We *know* what a good husband should look like/do, what a good Christian should act like/do, what a good mother should be/do, don't we? It was in the Perfect Person Memo. I hope you got it. If you had read the fine print, you'd know that when you mess up, you pay up. And more importantly, if you catch someone else messing up, you can make *him* pay. Unless the offending person is bigger than you; then you need to find a cat to kick.

> My wife doesn't care what I do when I'm away, as long as I don't have a good time.
>
> —LEE TREVINO

3. God doesn't (won't, can't) care about (for) you. It's hard to imagine that God would choose you to be on his team, isn't it? In fact, you ought to be grateful just to be saved. And since God is God, he can do whatever he pleases. You're a wriggling worm dangling over the fires of Hades. Get used to it.

4. It is hopeless. In fact, God is probably sick and tired of your whining and complaining. Not only that, you keep promising to get better, but look at you—wallowing in the same mud. Not only are you not worth God's love, grace, help, or kindness, you probably won't ever be. You'll never lose the weight, find a mate, quit drinking, smoking, gambling, gossiping, or cussing. The situation is hopeless—it'll never change. *You* are hopeless. Just give up.

> If at first you don't succeed, find out if the loser gets anything.
>
> —WILLIAM LYON PHELPS

When listed in black-and-white, the ridiculousness of these lies is blindingly obvious. Yet there just might be a sting in the heart, an involuntary sad nod of the head, or a tear in the eye. That's because we have *believed* these lies on some deep, inner level. It doesn't matter that they are so easily shot down; we continually fall into the trap of swallowing them on a day-to-day, what-if basis.

Let's go back through the above-mentioned lies again.

1. God has certain standards, and you don't meet them. Just this week, I found myself in a room full of Christians. They looked sharp and together. I had pulled on sweats and an old denim shirt because . . . that's just what I did. So. There. Most times, I don't mind my wardrobe, but on certain days, in specific situations, with particular (mostly Christian) people, it wouldn't matter if I had an outfit made by Diane Von Furstenberg herself; I feel like a piece of frump. And my reaction to feeling like there are standards and I'm not meeting them is to become defensive and fearful. *What if they really do look the way Christians are supposed to look, and . . . well, here I am? What if they don't like me because I'm dressed this way? Well, they won't ever like me, because this is just how I am! They probably think I'm a blob/slob/loser—see how that one talked to me? I don't fit in here—that's obvious. Blah, blah, blah.*

> I base my fashion taste on what doesn't itch.
>
> —GILDA RADNER

2. There are consequences when certain perfect standards aren't met. When expectations of the wouldacouldashoulda sort aren't met, there is some unwritten rule that a cat must be kicked. Think about a time when you were disappointed as a kid. Was it when it rained at your ninth birthday party? when you lost the basketball championship? when your dad/friend didn't do (or forgot to do or wouldn't do) something? How did you respond? Did you feel irritated? angry? sad? Maybe you went home and took out your negative emotions in the traditional American way, by smacking the daylights out of your little brother.

But what about now? When things don't go the way you'd planned, do you fret and fume? Do you hold it in until something small happens—like your kid or your spouse messes up or your coworker makes a small error—and then *kablooey!* You blow up like Mount St. Helens, spewing tons of verbal lava all over them?

3. God doesn't care about you (or doesn't care enough to get involved in your life). The thought process goes like this: *God doesn't care, because if he did, things (or my life) would look differently. My prayers would be answered (or the desires of my heart would get noticed or I'd find a spouse or have a baby or get a great job . . .).* Personally, I think this lie sets us up to feel isolated, vulnerable, and self-righteous. Each time the Creator doesn't follow our scripts on how things ought to go, we collect more damning evidence against him. Such logic in another context might look like a grain of sand condemning the ocean because the grain of sand found itself on a beach in New England instead of Hawaii.

> I don't know what your problem is, but I bet it's hard to pronounce.
>
> —SEEN ON A T-SHIRT

We somehow end up subconsciously thinking that *we* can determine whether what God does for us passes muster or not. Like Simon Cowell, the tart-tongued judge on *American Idol*, says, "He won't be winning this competition. You heard it here first." We don't reject God overtly, of course, because we're afraid we'll get a well-placed lightning bolt between the eyes. But we do it deep down. And at that moment, consciously or not, we place ourselves above God.

Imagine that the spaghetti you made for dinner sat up and said, "You've never done anything for me, so I'm not going to deal with you." This experience would provide you with several opportunities: 1) some excellent reasons to seek psychiatric help; 2) an option for extra cash by selling your chatty 'ghetti on eBay next to the French fry shaped like Abe Lincoln (OK—so the freaky fry was a prop and was actually put on Yahoo!auctions and brought in over $75,000 for charity[2]); and 3) fame (and possibly fortune) by selling your story to the *National Enquirer* and then charging admission for an audience with the famous Plate o' Pasta Prophet.

Regardless of what your spaghetti dinner *ever* says, you are still its creator. You can do anything you deem best for your creation, including eat it. God's like that. (In case you can't tell from this particularly unfortunate analogy, God is you and you is the 'ghetti.) It doesn't matter what *we* think about God or what approval rating we give him; he's the Creator, and we're the created.

Does that mean God doesn't care? No, he cares a lot—sending Jesus is undeniable proof of that. Consider this: for which strand of spaghetti would you sacrifice your only child? 'Nough said. But God also cares for you in a hundred ways a day. Stop and think about all the good things in your life like ice cream, sunsets, and nontalking Italian food. Even so, God's not required to obey us or coddle us. We are the spaghetti—ultimately we're to serve the maker.

4. It's hopeless. Any of the above lies always ends here.

GOD'S PURE TRUTH

Of course, there is some truth to each of those lies. Let's go through them one more time, break them down still further, and look for the pure truth (PT).

1. God does *have certain standards.* This is PT. Read the Old Testament and that's obvious. And while you're reading, notice how well the Hebrews followed the direct injunctions from the Almighty. As just one typical and graphic example, read in Exodus 32 about how Moses had hardly gone up the mountain for the Ten Commandments when God's chosen people decided to hold the first, and perhaps the only, Jewish Mardi Gras.

2. And you don't meet them. Of course we can't keep up with God's standards. Duh! If we could, we wouldn't need Jesus. And the Bible is pretty clear about that (Romans 3:9-20 and 5:12 for starters). All this is PT. But often the subtle message the enemy (and lots of people, including ourselves) implies is that we *should* somehow be able to meet God's standards (and probably everyone else's besides). Since we don't meet the standards, we must be defective losers. Here's where the first drop of poison is added to the PT water! The truth? Not being able to meet God's standards is *expected and normal.* The idea that our value is based on overcoming this natural order of things is a lie from the pit of Hell.

That's like saying a cabbage is bad because it's a cabbage. It is what it is. You don't have to personally enjoy eating anything with cabbage in it, but that doesn't make it inherently evil. It's just a cabbage.

> It's not whether you win or lose, it's how you place the blame.
>
> —OSCAR WILDE

3. *There are consequences when God's standards aren't met.* More PT. These consequences of our sin put Jesus on the cross (Romans 5:12; 1 Peter 2:24; 1 John 2:1, 2). And in life there are logical consequences: Smoking brings with it the real possibility of cancer. Eating nothing but Ho-Hos, Twinkies, and Big Macs brings the strong likelihood of obesity, heart disease, and diabetes (but what a way to go!). Unfortunately, there are also some consequences related to human ideals. You may have high expectations for yourself or family, your mother may be demanding, your boss might be considered difficult . . . What if these standards are not met? Should there be repercussions? What type, and who gets to decide?

FYI, the Bible doesn't say, "Love your *parents* with all your heart and with all your soul and with all your mind and with all your strength" (see Luke 10:27). And the verses about honoring your parents and about slaves obeying their masters aren't licenses for abuse. Yet with unbiblical, unrealistic expectations, another dropper of strychnine is added to the PT water.

We spend so much time trying to deal with the emotional consequences of other people's expectations, we forget that *God's* standards—the ultimate eternal requirements—have *already been satisfied* through Jesus Christ. Period. And since the hereafter is what really matters, the here and now can be treated as it truly is: a training camp, a development center, a kindergarten for the everlasting.

> If at first you don't succeed, blame your parents.
> —MARCELENE COX

4. God doesn't care about you. This is the summation of a long line of faulty logic that goes: *God is God. He can do what he wants. I am small and worthless. God doesn't have to care about me; he will do what he wants regardless of me. Actually, God doesn't care about me because of (fill in the blanks of disappointments or frustrations).*

Let's break this thought process down a bit: *God is God.* True. *I am small.* True. *And worthless.* FALSE! You are not *worthy*— meaning you don't deserve God's adoption—but you were so valuable that God sent his Son to die and thus redeem you (that is, buy you back) from the enemy. You may not be worthy of this act, but his doing it automatically makes you far from worthless. In fact, you are priceless. If you ever spend time in the I-am-worthless zone, add a tablespoon of poison to the glass.

5. God doesn't have to care about me. This could be true enough, except that he *does*—always has—to the point of making the earth for you (Genesis 1, 2), adopting you (when you decided to obey and follow him), and sending the Holy Spirit to live in you and help care for you. If you think God doesn't have to care or if you suspect he might not, add another glug of strychnine to the H_2O.

6. *He will do what he wants regardless of me.* The discussion of God's doing what he wants could make up another whole book. (Oh yeah—a sequel!) But you must understand that God doesn't just do what he wants like your cousin's bratty kid or your spouse or your evil little brother or your opportunistic boss or yourself . . . or whoever comes to mind when you think of selfish, egocentric people. God's goal is always the most loving thing for everyone, including you. However, the most loving thing from God's perspective (surprise!) might not include some of your wishes.

Bottom line: God wants everyone to grow up to be like his Son. If there is something you want that will help you do that, it seems God would probably be all over it. Everything else is either a maybe or a no. But if you measure God's love for you by how well he follows your script, add a big dose of strychnine, please.

7. *Actually, God doesn't care about me because* . . . Just toss in the rest of the bottle.

> I am, most definitely, Joy-impaired.
>
> —Matt Proctor

8. *It is hopeless.* Without Jesus, this statement is absolutely true. But it's surprising how often and convincingly I say it—even though I am a Christian with the Holy Spirit living in me, working to deal with the gunk in my life. By buying into this lie,

I put myself above God . . . or at least I try to take his place. When I declare that something is hopeless, I have decided that I know the situation better than an all-knowing, all-seeing, ever-present, not-bound-by-time-or-space (or calories) God, which then cancels out what Jesus did and denies the work of the Holy Spirit in my life. POISON! POISON! (*MWEEP! MWEEP!*) The water is now a toxic dump!

THE DOWNWARD SPIRAL

Every day, hundreds of times a day, we move from truth to untruth to total lie in a split second.

What does that have to do with the what-ifs? First of all, the what-ifs and maybes feed the lies. They are like yummy, high-calorie snack foods (emotional Ho-Hos, nachos grande, and Butterfingers) that seem at first bite to be no big deal but are, overall, deadly—if not immediately (as for a person who has diabetes), then eventually, by clogging arteries and increasing cellulite.

For instance, you might ask yourself questions like: *What if I don't fit in with these church people? Maybe I don't fit in because I'm a freak (and if I'm a freak, I can't be loved).* Or, *What if God really does whatever he wants regardless of me? Maybe that's how God is, and I'm just left here to figure out this mess by myself.* Or, *What if my prayers aren't being answered because he doesn't really care about me? My prayers aren't bad or selfish; they're for my sick child (or needed job or my friend); maybe God doesn't care about me or my kid. That would be my luck anyway—sucker me in to this Christian thing and then leave me in the lurch like all those other people did after they said they loved me.* (What is a lurch anyway?)

☕ SOOTHING INTROSPECTION

A Quick Review

Do any of these phrases sometimes run around in your head?

____ God has certain standards, and I obviously don't meet them.

____ There are consequences when certain standards aren't met. Someone needs to pay.

____ God doesn't care about me, really.

____ It is (and I am) hopeless.

____ Other _____

How often does this happen?

____ Rarely

____ Weekly

____ Daily

____ The lies are having dinner up in my head, and I'm the turkey.

____ You mean you can shut this stuff off? ☕

I had always viewed God as the Huge Guy, who wanted all words associated with him capitalized; who's really creative (just hang out in the Rocky Mountains or with a freshly diapered newborn); who has a wacky, and perhaps twisted, sense of humor (note duck-billed platypus and Hollywood as just two examples); who might be helpful if you begged hard enough (and hadn't been too bad); but who's a tad moody (note his conversations with Abraham and Moses concerning Sodom and Israel, respectively); and who's easily ticked off (again, see the Israelites or most any chapter in the Old Testament).

In the Gospel According to Marcy, God sent Jesus—and don't get me wrong, I am *extremely* grateful he did—but it seemed kind of obligatory: "Well, these folks can't get *anything* right, Son. You're going to have *show* them. Sheesh, you'd think they came from *monkeys* the way they act down there."

So Jesus heads our way. Saving us was his duty. And me dolefully serving him is mine (motto: Punch the clock and don't get caught).

My view of God was based on at least two untruths: 1) God noticed what I did *wrong*, not what I did *well*; and 2) I'm only on Jesus' team because he had to take me—(*I* picked *him*)—not because he would have chosen me. These fed into the lie that God doesn't really care for me and, therefore, can't be trusted.

> The advantage of the emotions is that they lead us astray.
>
> —Oscar Wilde

It got worse, but being a caring and sensitive writer, I'll spare you the details. When God finally gave me a glimpse of what I really thought about him . . . ewww! It was the black hole of me-ness. And even though I said all the correct Christian words in the correct spiritual order, they still pointed to the same center: me. My wants. My needs. My hurts. My healing. You'd think it would get crowded with all of those ids and egos. But no, we were an enmeshed little wad—me, myself, and I—covered by a self-protecting force field of pity and shame.

CHOOSING TO ACCEPT TRUTH

The truth? (And let me warn you—it may sound trite and cheesy, but I can't find a way to refute it.) It's not all about me. It can't be. I'm too small. It—life, the universe, and everything—needs to be all about someone greater, the maker, the giver of all good things; it's got to be about God. And we really don't have to do anything to help God be God. He's fully capable on his own. Joseph Mankiewicz said, "The difference between life and the movies is that a script has to make sense, and life doesn't." God's not required to follow my script, give in to my pouts, or earn my respect. That means I can look at him differently—with less expectation baggage blocking my vision. When life's not all about me, God can be God, even in my life.

TAKE YOUR MEDS

Memorize John 8:31, 32, 34-36:

"Jesus said, 'If you hold to my teaching, you are really my disciples. Then you will know the truth, and the truth will set you free.' . . . 'I tell you the truth, everyone who sins is a slave to sin. Now a slave has no permanent place in the family, but a son belongs to it forever. So if the Son sets you free, you will be free indeed.'"

We try to keep Jesus (and God) in tight quarters because we can't imagine them any other way. That's like a newly married couple whose bride refuses to open any of the wedding gifts or let her bridegroom change out of his tux—ever—because she loves thinking about that wonderful wedding day.

This woman is missing not only a few marbles but, more importantly to this example, the many expensive gadgets that come in handy during daily life. And she's missing the many wonderful facets (and outfits) a husband can have. It wouldn't take long for the tux to become soiled, stinky, and nasty—not to mention the huge late fee at the rental shop. By being unwilling to move on to the next level of the relationship . . . the bride would be labeled a total psycho. We are often like that bride. *If God isn't who I think he is, then what? What will he do? What will he make me do?* If our self-designed God-paradigm shatters, we reason, so will our world.

> The way it is now, the asylums can hold the sane people but if we tried to shut up the insane we should run out of building materials.
>
> —MARK TWAIN

Just as I remain Marcy Bryan regardless of who or what you wish me to be, God remains who he truly is regardless of what I call him, who I think he is, or how I choose to see and relate to him. *I'm* the one missing out on knowing my Father—he already knows all about me. And in the same way that you won't get to know the deep wonder that is my Marcy-fullness if you don't spend time with me, you don't (or won't) know God for who he is unless you spend time with him. Worst of all, it's not only your loss spiritually; it tends to affect how you handle every aspect of life and might even affect the way your children will handle their lives. But hey, no pressure.

> If you don't take me to the zoo, I'll change my name to Karen.
>
> —MEGHAN BRYAN (AT AGE FOUR)

⊘ SWEATLESS EXERCISE

Crack the Books

In order for me to begin seeing God differently, I gathered descriptions of him by others. C. S. Lewis, Max Lucado, early Calvin Miller books, and G. K. Chesterton were very helpful. Reading through the psalms and making a list of how God is described is also a good exercise. Assignments like these can refocus perspective. Let's say you decided to buy a yellow car because it's rare (and you like the color yellow). Once you've had that thought, you suddenly see a bazillion yellow cars on the road. Other cars seem to repaint themselves before your eyes. It's amazing! And once you start looking for other facets of God, you'll start seeing yellow cars too. No wait! Actually, you'll begin to notice other cool stuff about God that's been there all the time. I did. ⊘

Although I do not really want to, we need to now discuss . . . choice. It's not that I am against having options, especially when it comes to dark chocolate versus Brussels sprouts or lying around reading a favorite book versus doing dishes. But I suddenly become a helpless, drooling, angry mass when it comes to making potentially serious, healthful decisions. For instance, eating a bag of freshly opened potato chips versus a handful of old celery and carrots. Hmm. There is no choosing here. I can't help it. Must. Eat. Chips. AND. BAG. TOO. See?

Same with exercising. I have absolutely no time or oomph (the technical term for "get up and go") to do this, even if it's on my list or someone pays me. I do everything else but.

On second thought, getting paid *could* help. Send your generous donations to See! Me! Sweat! Pay me enough, and I'll do *your* workout for you. Spa slave, that'll be me! But unless someone is paying me or my mother is making me, I feel completely unable to pull away from the tyranny that is my life simply to walk around the block.

> We can try to avoid making choices by doing nothing, but even that is a decision.
>
> —GARY COLLINS

Realizing that attitudes and reactions are made up of many choices can really be depressing. It seems to me (using my own thought processes as a well-studied example) that I *truly* can't help my attitudes and reactions. Teach Meghan? *Someone has to.* Do laundry? *Let me ask this instead: Got underwear?* What's for dinner? *Who will slave away to make the ramen noodles or call Papa John's Pizza?* Be afraid? *It's just who I am.* See what I mean? I feel that my choices are pretty limited.

But if you look at self-help books or have friends in multilevel marketing or have been in sales or have a mom who is a famous motivational speaker, you know there are tons of people who think that attitude and choice go hand in hand, and—get this—they (attitude and choice) are your responsibility!

To put it a more guilt-inducing way: Nazi concentration camp survivor Victor Frankl wrote, "We who lived in concentration camps can remember the men who walked through the huts comforting others, giving away their last piece of bread. They may have been few in number, but they offer sufficient proof that everything can be taken from a man but one thing: the last of the human freedoms—to choose one's attitude in any given set of circumstances, to choose one's own way."[3]

At the risk of sounding totally heartless concerning Mr. Frankl—I'm not sure I can choose my attitude. And here's why: It seems to me that attitude seeps out from within an innermost site, a bottommost spot, an emotional bowel, if you will, which is . . . my caffeine gland. I'm joking! It's really the deep place where we determine our core beliefs.

Yet experience has taught me (although I'm an extremely slow learner) that I can consciously determine *what I believe.* So (using previous pathetically trite examples) if I choose to believe that potato chips are not as bad for me as people say, that will affect my preference of chips over carrots. Let's take the other thorn in my side: If I choose to believe that exercise is vital to my well-being as opposed to being just an item on my list each day, I will get my sorry self outside for some fresh air and calorie busting. Or if my doctor said I have to exercise or die, suddenly my beliefs would dramatically shift, which would alter my attitudes and cause me to become the Kickboxing Queen, the Thighmaster Master . . .

> Seize the moment. Remember all those women on the *Titanic* who waved off the dessert cart.
>
> —ERMA BOMBECK

Altering a belief often (although not always) goes beyond and below your emotions. You may need to employ your steel-jawed, nonfeeling will to this task. And let me tell you, your will loves to show off its steel-like jaw muscles. The change that comes out of an alteration of belief might initially appear exceedingly undramatic, but it's the only type of modification that seems to actually last.

> Anyone can conquer fear by doing the things he fears to do, provided he keeps doing them until he gets a record of successful experience behind him.
>
> —ELEANOR ROOSEVELT

Let's go back to our little lies. Many (probably all) of my negatively motivated actions have come from what I have believed about God, myself, and our relationship. If I absorb an untruth about God (*He won't take care of me*), myself (*I'm worthless*), and our relationship (*It's hopeless*), then my responses, attitudes, and actions will reflect those beliefs—usually ending up in fear, defensiveness, anger, depression, or something equally useful for initiating a breakdown.

However, I can believe the truth about God (*He's way bigger, stronger, wiser, and more caring than I can ever imagine; that's why he's called The All Mighty)*; about myself (*I'm not worthy of God's love, but he gives it to me anyway—and it's this love that makes me far from worthless!*); and about our relationship (*Christ died so I could have intimate interaction with the Creator, who is now my Father. That's COOL, and I want to get to know him more!*). If I do believe his truth, then my interaction with people, my reactions to situations, and my responses to my own actions will be directly affected. My attitudes will reflect my core beliefs.

The more I absorb PT, the less I find myself afraid. I don't worry that I'll fail, because God gets to say whether what I do equals success or failure. If I'm drawn closer to God through a situation, no matter how negative, God could consider the experience a success—his goal for my life might be for me to simply allow myself to be as intimate with him as possible.

When I believe God loves me and that he gets to say, I don't traumatize when people reject me, because I have the acceptance of the only one who matters forever. Shame thus loses its power.

> How bold one gets when one is sure of being loved!
> —SIGMUND FREUD

I might *feel* afraid or sad or angry, but these emotions won't dominate my daily thought processes or my interactions with people or situations. I believe God is on my side, and he will take care of whatever is going on—I don't have to.

And finally, death isn't a threat. While living, I'm in the process of becoming like my big brother Jesus and learning to love my Father. Death isn't the end; it means I finally get to go Home.

> It's great to be here. It's great to be anywhere.
> —KEITH RICHARDS'S REGULAR GREETING AT
> ROLLING STONES CONCERTS

You see, when I *believe*—or choose to believe, or try to choose to believe—the truth, I don't have to try to adjust my attitude; my emotions are not a factor, and circumstances aren't an issue. By continually selecting truth, things become changed at a subatomic level, beginning at my unseen, teeny spiritual DNA.

So was Viktor Frankl wrong? Absolutely not. I think what he saw as attitude was really belief. Anyone who would share his last piece of bread when he himself was starving, or could comfort people as he suffered in such hellish conditions, must have *truly believed* that hope was worth the effort and that there was something in a person that made him worthy of care.

I would like to say that these concentration camp prisoners understood God in a profound and amazing way, but I don't know that. I do know this: in order for those people to sustain a full cup during such obscene atrocities, they had to have something figured out at the deepest core of their beings.

TAKE YOUR MEDS

Memorize the words Jesus spoke to the synagogue ruler in Mark 5:36: *"Don't be afraid; just believe."*

The more we choose to believe the truth, the more we will notice that the things, activities, and situations that felt (scientifically speaking) stressful feel (once again we look to the scientific community) nonstressful. Eventually we may come to a crossroads. Down one lane we see that by doing the same old things as before, the road leads back to the pit of fear, depression, and other yucky things. The other road may seem more difficult, and even bumpier initially, but that's because it's not been used as much.

Let's recap:

- God gets to say.
- He's way bigger, stronger, wiser, and more caring than I can ever imagine; that's why he's called The All Mighty.
- We can choose to believe truth.
- Believing truth makes all the difference!
- *Recap* is a fun word to say.

1. Grab your notebook and record one thought about this chapter, one positive thing that happened today, one Scripture that you like, and one way that God has blessed you.

2. What struck you as interesting or unusual in this chapter? Why?

3. Choose one Scripture that you will try to memorize. Write it down.

4. Look back at the four basic lies. Which one do you most identify with today? Can you explain why?

5. In your opinion, is there a difference between attitude and belief? Explain. If there's a dictionary nearby, look up each word. Do the definitions help?

6. Try a unique way to describe how you view God. For example, how would you describe him in terms of color? It sounds corny, but try it anyway. Write and finish sentences like: Green reminds me of God because . . . Red reminds me of God because . . .

   Remember to check the Resources section on page 247.

AN iSSUE OF TRUST

In God we trust, all others pay cash.

—SEEN ABOVE A CAFÉ CASH REGISTER IN SOUTH DAKOTA

The lies floating around in our heads are looking for places to move into, raise a family, and maybe retire. They have one goal—to separate us from God and to damage our relationship with him. Um, OK . . . the lies we believe have two goals—to separate us from God and damage our relationship with him, and to prevent us from seeing who we are in Christ. Er . . . correct that. The lies we believe have *many* goals, some of which include: separating us from God, damaging our relationship with him, preventing us from seeing who we are in Christ, and persuading us to reject the blessings the Holy Spirit wants to give us as he lives inside us. Whew!

When I feel as if I can't let Meghan do something (like go on a field trip) because I'm afraid of what might happen to her, what am I really saying about God? *He won't take care of my daughter. He's not trustworthy.*

Granted, we're presuming the activity has plenty of trained, responsible chaperones who have left their résumés and cell phone numbers with me. We reasonably expect that the genders shalt be always separated and that the abovementioned chaperones will drive 5 mph less than the posted speed limit and that they (the children and adults) will all be tucked in their respective beds by 10:45 PM with teeth brushed and braces flossed.

I know what you're thinking. Yes, it *is* amazing that I can have all of these requirements and still be the hippest parent I know. My daughter, however, would rather I not say the word *hip,* because apparently there's this Universal Coolness Factor (UCF), and using words like *hip, groovy,* and *rad* proves I have cobwebs hanging off my nose, hideously colored polyester clinging to my legs, and comical batwing glasses flapping off my face—that only people of a certain age can see.

It's kind of like the cell phone rings that teenagers are using, which are the same pitch as dog whistles. Apparently, only pooches and pre-adults can hear these sounds, while their geriatric educational instructors and older-than-dirt parents cannot. As far as I can tell, my current UCF is a minus 5 and dropping like a stone. I guess this means I'm a healthy, normal parent.

> You know your children are growing up when they stop asking you where they came from and refuse to tell you where they're going.
>
> —P. J. O'ROURKE

I don't fly well. Mike Harding advises: "If forced to travel on an airplane, try and get in the cabin with the Captain, so you can keep an eye on him and nudge him if he falls asleep or point out any mountains looming up ahead." When I struggle to ride in an airplane or feel distressed and panicky while away from home, what am I saying about God? *He might not keep me safe.* And being safe is seemingly the most important thing to me. Since I cannot be guaranteed safety at *all* times, God cannot be trusted.

When I feel rejected by a friend or family member and just want to run away or eat too much or drink too much or whatever . . . what am I saying about God? *Pain is bad. God didn't prevent this from happening, which means I must take care of the pain myself because he won't or can't. God isn't my advocate; therefore, God cannot be trusted.*

SOOTHING INTROSPECTION

Make a Meds List (see "The Enemy's Plan" page 112)

Please list how you medicate—if you dare! (Note: Even good things count.)

What do you do to make yourself feel better when you've had a bad day?

Do you eat or drink certain things when you feel overwhelmed? Or do you *do* something instead?

Try to be brutally honest.

And then go have some chocolate. You know what Abraham Lincoln said: "It has been my experience that folks who have no vices have very few virtues."

When I fail and fall (one more time), tsunamis of hopelessness sweep over my soul, and I believe my life, my marriage, my struggle, and my fears will never get better—not even with a miracle direct from the Almighty himself. I thus brand myself a miserable loser with a neon green *L* stamped on my forehead for all to see. What am I saying about God in that moment? *He doesn't know enough. He doesn't know* me *well enough. I know better.* And I get to say what a loser looks like—where's that mirror again? It becomes all about me, a little *g* god in my universe-swallowing me-ness. *God is obviously a liar—he cannot be trusted.*

When my heart has been mauled and God seems silent—when the what-if actually happens—and I seriously think Job's wife had it right after all (that I should just curse God and die), what am I saying about God? I'm making my script more important than his plan. *He should have done something that would have been good and pleasing in my sight. And since he didn't, it must mean he wasn't there or didn't care or* (worse yet) *willed it to happen. See? I told you God couldn't be trusted.*

GOD'S PLAN

For several months one of Kevin's brothers, whom we'll just call David, lived with us. Meghan was four, and she loved Uncle David. It came to pass that, to follow God's leading and go back to school, David had to leave our nurturing and delightful presence. Megh was devastated.

We tried to explain David's move in the context of God's plan. One day Megh commented, "I still don't think I like God's plan for Uncle David because David had to leave. I miss him so much. *Gasp!* You don't think Uncle David *wanted* to leave? Because if he wanted to leave us, then that would hurt my heart more than God's plan. My heart would be so broken it would look like cookie crumbs, but tinier and probably red and dripping with tears."

Isn't this how we often feel? Well, you may be *way* more together, but this is certainly how *I* feel sometimes. *Please let this be a mistake*, part of me begs. *Please don't let this be your will.* Yet another side of me knows that God is aware of everything. This doesn't help. In my warped and aching mind, his apparent lack of intervention only proves his delinquency.

Why does an understanding of God's plan matter so much? Because our ideas about relationships are pretty messed up, that's why. And because our relationship with God is the primary reason we exist. The answer to the *Westminster Shorter Catechism*'s first question ("What is the chief end of man?") is summed up this way: "Man's chief end is to glorify God, and to enjoy him forever."[1] We really need to get this.

Of course, you've heard the verse "For God so loved the world that he gave his one and only Son, that whoever believes in him shall not perish but have eternal life" (John 3:16). That word *loved* is from the Greek word *agape*, which doctors of divinity tell us is a picture of loving in a willful, devoted, gracious, and giving way.

You might feel this way toward a friend or even someone who works for you, but you'd probably experience this type of emotion most often in a family or see it in a devoted couple married a long time. (*Long time* here means for more than, say, eight years, if you use the reported average length of a typical US marriage as being between four and seven years—which is, according to the US Department of Justice, about the average duration of a prison sentence.[2]) This *agape* love is when you are able to sit in the same room, each doing his or her own thing but feeling a closeness, a sweetness, a safeness, and a sense of unity.

What is the chief goal of man? When Jesus was asked about the most important commandment, he actually gave two. The first: "Love [*agape*] the Lord your God with all your heart and with all your soul and with all your mind and with all your strength." And the second: "Love [*agape*] your neighbor as yourself" (Mark 12:30, 31). To me, Jesus is saying that I love God by purposefully choosing to show that I love him through prayer and worship; by being generous and devoted in the way I use my time and resources; by learning about God so as to be comfortable enough to share my dreams, fears, and thoughts; and by learning through experience to enjoy (and trust) him and his kindness and gifts. This, then, allows me to love others in the same way. This is God's plan. Do I always follow it? Um . . . I have to go now.

TAKE YOUR MEDS

Toby Green said, "My goal in life is to become as wonderful as my dog thinks I am." God is much more wonderful than we think he is. There are many verses describing God's desire to have a relationship with us. See how many you can find. Here are a few to get you started:

"Obey me, and I will be your God and you will be my people. Walk in all the ways I command you, that it may go well with you" (Jeremiah 7:23).

"Is God the God of Jews only? Is he not the God of Gentiles too? Yes, of Gentiles too" (Romans 3:29).

"Consider Abraham: 'He believed God, and it was credited to him as righteousness.' Understand, then, that those who believe are children of Abraham. The Scripture foresaw that God would justify the Gentiles by faith, and announced the gospel in advance to Abraham: 'All nations will be blessed through you.' So those who have faith are blessed along with Abraham, the man of faith" (Galatians 3:6-9).

THE ENEMY'S PLAN

The devil, as God's enemy, has goals for us as well, which can be summed up in this mature way: If God has something, then by golly, his enemy wants it too. Or if the enemy can't have it, then he wants to destroy it so that God can't have it either. So if you're going to have an enemy, try to have a grown-up one and not one that sounds like a spoiled five-year-old, is what I say.

Since having a relationship with you is important enough for God to send his Son, you and your relationship with God are important enough to be attacked. How does God's enemy try to drive a wedge between God and his children? He uses tools, of course. Some of these are obvious, and some may surprise you; but all seem to be astoundingly effective. Let's look at a few of the more common ones.

We've already talked about how the injudicious use of media will add boatloads of swill to your thought life. Therefore, I can definitely and scientifically say that God's enemy could find this a useful tool.

And we've also discussed how people can negatively affect and annoy us. Oscar Wilde illustrates (in reference to some unnamed person): "He has no enemies, but is intensely disliked by his friends." Human interaction at its redeemed best is a beautiful shadow of our relationship with God, our oneness through Jesus, and our vitality as the body and bride of Christ. When it's good, it's heavenly.

But when interpersonal relationships go south, it's painful and traumatizing. Most people who reject Christianity do so not because of Jesus, but because someone who claimed to be a Christian abused them, was mean to them, used them, rejected them, or somehow hurt them badly.

> Never interrupt your enemy when he is making a mistake.
>
> —NAPOLEON BONAPARTE

Speaking of hurting, chocolate can be a tool of the devil. OK, not *just* chocolate but anything we eat, drink, or do that takes the place of dealing with our cruddy emotions and the lies we believe that keep God at arm's length. What's your poison? Diet Coke? Shopping? People? Chocolate? Being "busy"? Movie watching? Chips? Wine? Running? Smoking? Internet "research"? Pizza Hut Double Stuffed Crust? What do you reach for when life gets to be too much? Perhaps you imitate Karen Salmansohn: "I try to fill the emptiness deep inside me with Cheetos, but I am still depressed. Only now my fingers are stained orange. I am blue. And I am orange."[3]

Whatever it is, the proper name for it is medication. In the Bible it's called sin, but I hate to make myself and you, dear reader (who spent like, real money on this book), feel too badly. Some might call it an idol, but I don't like the sound of that either.

Whatever the name, the use is the same—we medicate, letting whatever it is take the place of God (see Exodus 20:3). We turn to these "medicines" to try to fill up that God-shaped hole and make ourselves feel better about something only God can.

SWEATLESS EXERCISE

Evil Media Activity

Take account of your media intake.

How many hours of TV do you watch in a week? ____

How many movies do you watch in a week? ____

How many hours of radio do you listen to in a week? ____

How long are you on the Internet each day? ____

What do you do there primarily?

____ Read the news

____ See what I can find

____ Research a particular interest

How much of what you see/listen to/read/find would you consider to be stress filled?

____ Some

_____ Half

_____ Most

What type of TV shows do you watch? Circle all that apply.

News

Sitcoms

Reality-type shows (*Survivor*)

Contest-type shows (*American Idol, Deal or No Deal*)

Dramatic thrillers (*Alias, Lost*)

Weather (TWC and its *Storm Stories*)

Cooking (*Iron Chef, Emril*)

Cop shows

Cartoons

Other: _____ 🌀

C. S. Lewis said, "Enemy-occupied territory—that is what this world is."[4] Not to be redundant, but let me say again: the enemy will use absolutely *anything*, especially good things like chocolate, Pizza Hut, and exercise, to draw us away from God.

And to be honest, medicating feels easier because the hurt is momentarily relieved, the wound is licked, the ouchie is bandaged (even though you're worse off in the long run). Falling into God's arms seems scary and unknown—*What might he make me do? What if I don't like it? What if it doesn't work?* (The what-ifs are back again!) Holding on to those things that are comforting seems safer, regardless of the truth that God is the very best at rescuing and healing. Whaddya know?! Another great reason to Read! Your! Bible!

TAKE YOUR MEDS

Read Ephesians 1:3-10 to get a glimpse of yourself and others through the Almighty's eyes. Write down any pertinent thoughts, specifically about ways in which God rescues his children. ◀▮

MY JOURNEY OF TRUST

Since trusting is good and medicating is bad, you might wonder how I am doing at the former versus the latter. I can confidently say I'm doing better. Mostly. And it started by telling God that I was medicating for relief instead of turning to him for rescue. That's it. OK, I did tell a few close fellow strugglers so they could pray for me as well (see James 5:16, though I'll talk directly about that verse in chapter 7).

Next, I began to examine what my drugs of choice really looked like. When did I feel the need to run away? What did I reach for when I felt stressed out? Wow, I was stunned at how many things had become druglike for me. And although I was still medicating more than meditating, I continued to confess this to God (and certain others), admitted I couldn't get better on my own, and asked for help (especially from God) and prayers (from friends).

Slowly he has drawn me closer, and I've let go of more. But I still medicate. When things get really bad and I'm up against the wall, I reach for something that makes me feel immediately better. In these moments especially, I'm very grateful God loves me. That's what the Bible says (see 1 John 4:7-21 as just one example), and I have to remind myself to believe this instead of my lying mind-tapes and deceiving feelings that continually try to convince me that the situation is hopeless and so am I.

TAKE YOUR MEDS

Go to biblegateway.com and look up these keywords:

"God, children" (you'll find John 1:12, 13; Romans 8:17-21; and others).

"God, love" (you'll find Ephesians 5:1, 2; Colossians 2:2; 1 John 3:1; and others).

Check out the verses you find. How does God see you? ◖▶

So I'm writing a book while I'm still walking through this struggle. Am I a hypocrite? I guess I could be. But I don't know—trying to willingly admit my faults even though I still have them actually makes me not a hypocrite by definition, according to the *Oxford English Dictionary*. But what, then, am I?

Let's make up a new idiomatic phrase to describe this state of being. Hmm . . . we'll call it grunge Christianity. It means trying to live honestly with self, God, and others—and not in a flaunty, self-righteous way. It's trying to be real like the Velveteen Rabbit. It's trying to be OK with self but not satisfied, understanding that today doesn't equal forever and that drawing closer to God is what I deeply want but can't do on my own. It's allowing God to love me without any yeah-buts and then trying to love others beyond their yeah-buts.

As a grunge Christian I can proclaim, "I'm just me, but according to God's Word, God loves me. And that's what Heaven and salvation and joy and all the other good stuff from God are totally about."

> If I were two faced, would I be wearing this one?
> —Abraham Lincoln

Will I always be fighting fear or struggling with my belief system? I have hope that maybe to an ever-increasing degree in this life (and totally and assuredly in the next!), I'll break free from all that hinders me.

But I'll probably have bits and pieces to work on all my days. I'm a human, after all, and limping along with my crippled self. Hauling along or peeling off some kind of junk is part of living. God's OK with that, and I need to be OK with it even as I'm not content with it.

FIGHTING ON THE RIGHT SIDE

The earlier listed medicinal things aren't hellishly bad—you can even do them and *still go to Heaven*. Not all are überhealthful, but they will not send you straight to Hell (first you have to go through New Jersey). Here's the kicker: you can even *enjoy* most of them and *still* be a Christian. How wild is that! It is entirely *how* they are used by you (or the enemy) that makes them good or evil. And often only you and God know which it really is.

One last tool the adversary can use to affect our relationship with God: ourselves. I don't know about you, but I really am my own worst enemy. In nanoseconds I'll judge and condemn my "sorry personage" to the sulfurous fires of Hades. Interestingly, I magnanimously offer most people in a similar position at least a thimbleful of grace. Yet for myself, I'll not only agree with the accuser's claims, I'll beat him to it! *Yup, I am a loser,* I mentally berate myself, wagging my sorrowful but knowing head. *No wonder no one loves me. I'm not even worth bothering with . . .* sniff, sniff. *Now where'd I put those Oreos?*

STRESS FREE QUIZ

You Call Yourself a *What?*

Groucho Marx said, "I refuse to join any club that would have me as a member." What do you call yourself when you make a mistake?

____ Precious ____ Loser ____ Dummy ____ Can't repeat it

What do you call your son/daughter/other family members when they do something you don't like?

____ Loser ____ Idjit ____ Sweet Chunks ____ Can't repeat it

Do you find yourself making fun of other people's weaknesses?

____ Yes, but only if it's really funny

____ No, not if it's really bad

____ Did you get a load of *her*?

When we agree with or assist the enemy, we are against God. Doesn't that make us enemies of God, unwitting though we may be? Thankfully, the Almighty appears to look at us in a manner similar to the way we look at our teenage children. They (the teens, ergo ourselves) can seem to be adversarial and perhaps even foe-like. "Most children threaten at times to run away from home," said Phyllis Diller. "This is the only thing that keeps some parents going."

But insightful, patient parents know that (or have a hope that) the teens aren't, for the most part, demonic. No matter what, they are still our kids, and we know who they are deep in their hearts. Eventually they will grow up and have babies of their own. They will then take the same "stupid pills" they think we have taken now. And we will laugh. God, similarly, sees our state of being but knows that this is not our DNA, it's not our true essence. We are still becoming. And I'm sure he's thankful.

As God's kids we must not side with our Father's foe—either by agreeing with his accusations about us and our Father or by doing what he wants. Listen to your mental (and verbal) conversations and see which side they represent. There's no neutral territory here. If you call yourself (or others) names, if you put yourself (or others) down, if you make fun of yourself (or others) in a way that is humiliating or cruel—you aren't being funny or a friend; you are being a tool of God's arch nemesis.

> We've seen the enemy, and he is us.
>
> —TOM RATH

You may need to consciously take notes concerning how you mentally refer to yourself. Use any popular note-taking technique, like sticky notes. It doesn't matter; you'll immediately lose them.

But it's a great way to feel official and useful at the time. Plus, if you jot things down rather than talk to yourself, it looks like you're some brilliant, creative type, instead of some disturbed, psycho type. So focus on (meaning "write down") what you say to yourself. Easy, you say? You're pretty relaxed about stuff, you claim? Listen closely to your mental tapes. Do you call yourself *idiot* more that *cool dude*? (By the way, everyone should call themselves *cool dude* for a month, especially in front of their children's friends. It's a humbling experience, and it'll embarrass your kids—what a great two-fer deal!) Taking a mental name-calling inventory was a stunning exercise for me. I couldn't believe what I called myself. If I were my own mother, I'd be washing my mouth out with soap. That's all I'm saying.

In case you're wondering, I'm not suggesting you should talk yourself into being something you are not. But I *am* saying don't curse yourself if God doesn't. Jesus said, "If the Son sets you free, you will be free indeed" (John 8:36). And Paul beats the topic into a froth in his letter to the Romans when he describes how one man's (Adam's) sin placed us all on the Guilty List, but one man (Jesus) supplied total absolution because he fit the requirements (Christ being perfect and God and all). Paul finishes it off by saying, "Therefore, there is now no condemnation for those who are in Christ Jesus" (Romans 8:1). Whoa. If God doesn't damn us, then maybe we should be careful to not damn ourselves either.

> It's too bad I'm not as wonderful a person as people say I am, because the world could use a few people like that.
> —ALAN ALDA

Agreeing with the enemy feeds any and all fears. *What if I foul this up?* you ask yourself. *Of course you will,* comes your immediate mental answer, *because you always do. You're a loser.* Or at a microscopic level, *What if I try this new menu item at Wendy's?* you think. *Why waste the five dollars?* comes your immediate response. *That's a lot of money for lunch. You can't afford it, even though it's the most healthful thing on the menu. Besides, you'll probably not like it anyway—you never like stuff like that (because you're a loser).*

When we agree with the accusations of the enemy and, specifically, when we join in by calling ourselves names, we: 1) immediately go against God, effectively telling him he doesn't know what he's talking about; 2) strip God of his majesty and power in our lives; 3) become blind to any activity God does do; and 4) commit spiritual suicide—verbally and mentally slashing ourselves bloody. Who needs Satan to beat us up? We quickly become very talented at stabbing our own sorry selves without him. Oops—I called us "sorry selves," just like he wanted. Open the floodgates, darlin', and let the fears pour in!

What can God do with an attitude like that? I suppose the best thing is to let us wallow in it until we are so tired of the nastiness, we let God actually be in charge of us. I don't know about you, but at this point I don't want to give the enemy any more ammo. And I have finally decided I don't want to try to be God—the hours are grueling and the pay stinks.

TAKE YOUR MEDS

Meditate on 1 John 4:7-11:

"My dear friends, we must love each other. Love comes from God, and when we love each other, it shows that we have been given new life. We are now God's children, and we know him. God is love, and anyone who doesn't love others has never known him. God showed his love for us when he sent his only Son into the world to give us life. Real love isn't our love for God, but his love for us. God sent his Son to be the sacrifice by which our

sins are forgiven. Dear friends, since God loved us this much, we must love each other" (CEV).

Memorize Proverbs 3:5, 6:

"Trust in the Lord with all your heart; do not depend on your own understanding. Seek his will in all you do, and he will direct your paths" (NLT). ◖◗

1. Grab your notebook and record one thought about this chapter, one positive thing that happened today, one Scripture that you like, and one way that God has blessed you.

2. What struck you as interesting or unusual in this chapter? Why?

3. Choose one Scripture that you will try to memorize. Write it down.

4. What tool does the enemy most often use to attack you? Why is that a strategic move on his part?

5. What's your favorite "medication"? Why?

6. Extra credit challenge: Read through the whole book of Ephesians (it's short), and see all that God has done for and through us. Use a highlight marker or make a list.

   Remember to check the Resources section on page 247.

THE PRICE
OF NON-TRUST

Fear is, I believe, a most effective tool in destroying
the soul.

—ANWAR EL-SADAT

OK, let's recap: Fears (and other negative attitudes and behaviors) have many factors and causes, but the deepest involve the effects of the lies we believe about ourselves and God. These lies hamstring, hinder, and then halt our kinship with our Father through a lack of trust. That's bad because this relationship happens to be the most important one in existence.

If trust is so important (and lack thereof so bad), then: A) why are we so pathetic at doing it; and B) why don't we talk about it?

The more people I meet, the more I like my dog.

Let's explore part B first, because I can guess at its answer. We'll call it an *educated* guess; that sounds more impressive. It's my extremely educated guess that we don't discuss our individual or collective lack of trust because the enemy is that sneaky. (Read C. S. Lewis's *The Screwtape Letters* for a clever account of how Satan might work.) Or perhaps people presume that faith and trust are so consummately linked—if you have one, you automatically have the same amount of the other.

Yet according to Romans 15:13, Paul blesses the Romans with joy and peace *as* they trust in God *so* they will overflow with hope and power; it was a perpetual process. Or maybe we don't talk about our lack of trust because we're all so bad at it, but we think we should be good at it and since we *should* be good at it and we're not, if we don't admit it we might be able to fake it and thus go through life semi-traumatized but not totally shame-faced. ("I mean . . . *really. You* don't trust the Creator of the universe? What's wrong with you? What? Do *I* really trust him? Well, *ahem* . . . I don't think I want to talk about it.")

> Heaven: A place where the wicked cease from troubling you with talk of their personal affairs, and the good listen with attention while you expound on yours.
>
> —Ambrose Bierce

So much for why we don't talk about it. Sorry I can't be more help. Let's go back to point A, why we don't *do* it—speaking of trusting, specifically.

IDENTITY ISSUES

One reason appears to be found within identity. Often we rely on our state of being to define who we are. For example,

I am Kevin's wife and Meghan's mom, as opposed to, let's say, being Queen Marcy of the Universe. My state of being—married, a mom, Little League coach, president of the Prune Board—provides a way to classify and define me. The longer a person abides in a certain state, the stronger the potential identity. I've been Kevin's wife for more than twenty years and Meghan's mom for well over a decade. If either of these situations were to change, I would feel out of sorts, wondering who I am.

Being fearful or angry or depressed is the same sort of identity. After a while this struggle is so much a part of you that you can't imagine being anything else. Be honest—who would you be if you were no longer a worrywart, stressed out, or depressed?

Is it hard to imagine? Sure, I *say* I want to be different, but when it comes down to actually doing something about it, or when it's time to show how the healing is going, I quickly pop back into my freaked-out, fear-filled mode because it's comfortable; I know what's required of me and how I'll react. The response "It's just who I am" (meaning that I believe this is who I will be *forever*) is a potent lie impressed on us by the enemy. And it's a lie that keeps us from trusting.

STRESS FREE QUIZ

Check Your ID

Marshall McLuhan said, "Canada is the only country in the world that knows how to live without an identity." But individuals seem to need one. How do you identify yourself? Check from this list and add more.

____ Parent

____ Sibling

____ Seller of Jelly Bellies

____ Owner of Starbucks (Please be my friend.)

How would your family identify you?

____ Mom/Dad

____ Moneybags

____ The one who's always running late

How would your friends identify you?

____ Chatterbox

____ Serious

____ Ditzy

____ Sports nut

Now fill in how God identifies you.

_____ (see Isaiah 43:4)

_____ (see John 15:13-15)

_____ (see Romans 8:16-18)

Although we might not say this to anyone, there is another list to add to the above quiz, isn't there? It's one that goes like this: *You're so disgustingly needy; who wants to be around you?* Or, *You're worthless, stupid, a total loser.* (These are mine. Feel free to construct your own.) I'm talking about lies we've believed so deeply and for so long that they feel like they're part of our personal makeup, our spiritual DNA.

It would be like growing up all your life thinking you were part of the Bryan family. Mom and Dad treated you as their child, and the kids reacted to you like a sibling. Even the extended family interacted as though you were a member of the family. One day you find a letter saying you were, in fact, adopted and that your birth parents live in Des Moines. (Look, if you want better stories you'll have to read Max Lucado.)

How would you feel now? If it were me . . . well, beyond the frustration and anger I might hold toward my present family for keeping this little tidbit a secret, and beyond the desire to know why my other parents put me up for adoption, I know what I would think: *Who do I look and act more like?* I would suddenly wonder, *Who am I? Really.*

Same with these deep-seated lies—giving them up sounds nice, but what will I be *then*? Listen in: *I've been depressed for years. What will I look like if every day is sunny? Can I even* stop *being a worrywart? Can I stop being fearful? You see, I* know *what fearful looks and feels like. So if I'm courageous . . . um, what will I have to do? Where will I have to go? What if . . . ?*

> We have normality. I repeat, we have normality. Anything you still can't cope with is therefore your own problem.
> —DOUGLAS ADAMS

Another identity issue that keeps us stuck in the negative zone of non-trust is being a victim. Victims believe that their lives are cruddy because of everything and everyone but themselves. If you play the victim, it will be most visible in the language you use describing yourself (or others). "This *always* happens to me." "See, I just *knew* I was jinxed!" Or in the immortal words of Rodney Dangerfield (I'm not that old, just well-versed in pop culture), "I get no respect!" Being a victim is very handy when a person is afraid of change, because it takes away one's perceived power. "I can't help it!" looks way better than "I could change. But I really like being miserable, so I'm just going to stay this way and pretend to want to change so you will pity me and take care of me, which will result in my not having to do any work!"

I found the victim role exceedingly convenient. It allowed me to whine and mope. (Groucho Marx had me pegged: "It isn't necessary to have relatives in Kansas City in order to be unhappy.") I pointed fingers at my husband, my daughter, my family, and my circumstances—proclaiming loudly that they were the reasons I couldn't accomplish brave, impressive things. Why I had to accomplish brave, impressive things still remains a mystery, but there you have it. Abandoning the poor-me syndrome is a huge step in changing one's future reactions and behavior. I'm not advocating that you "simply" pull yourself up by your bootstraps—I believe God has a huge hand in any serious emotional healing. But I am saying that we have to take responsibility for what is ours and learn to let go of what is not.

> Men and nations behave wisely once they have exhausted all the other alternatives.
>
> —ABBA EBAN

Years ago I read *Boundaries* by Drs. Cloud and Townsend. The word picture that sums up their excellent book is to liken a person's emotional, physical, and spiritual space to a yard.[1] Let's say each person is a nice patch of grass with a fence surrounding it. Mine has English yew hedges on the two sides; an open vista of mountains out in the back; and an artsy not-quite-picket fence and a gate with a high, flower-covered arch in front. (Who said fences had to be the same all around?) Oh, and a huge live oak with droopy limbs is in the middle of the yard, with patches of flowers and comfortable, picturesque places to sit scattered about liberally.

According to the good doctors, I am responsible for the condition and upkeep of my yard. However, sometimes people will come right up to my fence and dump their trash into my zone. These "boundary breakers" seem to expect me to take care of their stuff. A healthy person doesn't let people dump nastiness into his yard. Nor does he dump his nasties onto another's spot. When I am a "victim," I let people toss whatever they want over my fence until my precious bit o' green is ruined. That's not being a good gardener. Take responsibility and care for your area. Own up to what is yours, and encourage others to do the same.

CONTROL ISSUES

Another reason that non-trust seems so useful (and thus so difficult to give up) is that it appears to give us permission to do what we want. How about that for a deep, scientific analysis? When I am distressed, depressed, or dejected, I am free to do whatever helps take the pain away—medicate, protect myself, or lash out. I get to say. I'm judge and jury. But if I'm trusting God to take care of things, God is the one who gets to say. And medicating, withdrawing, and being witchy are not necessarily on the Approved Continued Reaction to Trauma List.

You see it happening all the time. Give toddlers a ball, and soon the "It's mine!" game starts. Tell a young child to do something, and "No!" is often the first response (or, "You're not the boss of me," if the little darling belongs to someone else). Later on, teenagers will do the Linda-Blair-*The-Exorcist* eye roll or the slamming-of-the-door salute to let you know they don't find your insightful input or pleasant request welcome. Adults might say yes but then quickly "forget" or stuff their real feelings until they blow up. Basically, we all want to be Most Supreme Semi-Benevolent Ruler of our little kingdoms, Emperor Caesar with some kind of absolute power resting on the tip of a thumb. And we'll do whatever it takes in order for it to stay that way. That's right, no one can tell *me* what to do. *I'm* the boss of me.

Staying in non-trust also lets me take control of situations and people. It's a case of the squeaky, crabby, traumatized wheel getting to make everyone else walk on eggshells around her, doing whatever it takes so that she will finally amp down and SHUT UP. If I am the center of all things, I can say what I want, go where I want, or stay home if I want. I can guilt, shame, badger, or abuse people into serving my needs because, as my dear friend Kathy jokingly says, "It's *always* all about me! You might as well know that right now."

> The squeaky wheel doesn't always get greased; it often gets replaced.
>
> —JOHN PEERS

Being in the state of non-trust gives me permission to *not* do things or *not* deal with certain people or situations as well. It's infinitely more convenient to be "stressed out" than to interact kindly, gently, and honestly with difficult people. (*Difficult people* here means those more irritating and/or obnoxious than me at the time.) It can seem safer not to let Meghan go on a trip with friends than to wrestle with the stress (and potential ramifications should something go wrong) of releasing her. (Releasing her also means that she's growing up and I'm getting old—two things I'd rather not deal with.) It's simpler to say "I can't/you can't" to something new, something out of my comfort zone, or something risky (no matter how slight the risk) than it is to embrace whatever adventure lies ahead with its complex emotions, unknown requirements, and potential growth.

> Both optimists and pessimists contribute to our society. The optimist invents the airplane and the pessimist the parachute.
>
> —G. B. STERN

If I do end up going and doing, I often "suddenly" have an upset stomach, chest pains, headache, and other symptoms from a generous dose of fight-or-flight hormones pumping through my system. On top of that I become prickly, meaning "very unpleasant to the point of actually growing spines and breathing fire."

Sure, I might like the event afterwards, but getting me there, kicking and screaming, is really no fun, particularly for the one who is persuader and transporter of porcupiney me. Kev has declined many opportunities for enjoyment and adventure rather than have to "pay the price of admission" by convincing me that the potential event (my interpretation of which was "trauma") might be fun. Thus I make him (or anyone else) pay for stretching me. *Bwa-ha-ha-ha-ha!* (That's evil, mad scientist laughter—if you're not a science-fiction movie buff.) With my supreme whinyness and sharp tongue, I have power over all who dare disturb my comfort zone. Cower before me, mere mortals!

Frying Eggs with God

In his book entitled *Lifetime Guarantee* and video series called The Life, Christian psychologist Bill Gillham makes a great point about giving God the power to say what is a success or failure. Both of these are *excellent* resources for grace and growth. The following is my paraphrase of one of his terrific illustrations[2] (and is probably extremely loose. Sorry, Bill).

Let's say you want to honor God in all that you do, so while making breakfast you decide to fry some eggs using the power of the Holy Spirit. You've always had trouble flipping the eggs in the pan and keeping the yolks intact. This morning, you decide to give this activity to God. You slip your spatula under the egg and . . . yee-haw! Perfect flip! Perfect egg! Go God!

Next morning. Same scenario. Give it to God. Flip the egg. Perfect egg! Yeah God!

Third morning. One more time. You give it to God, and you carefully flip the egg . . . but this time the yolk breaks and makes a mess everywhere.

Here's the question: On day three did you fail? Did God? If God gets to say what is success and failure, and presuming you gave yourself to him as best you could, then shouldn't *he* say whether the moment was a boom or a bust? Unlike us, he seems more interested in our leaning on him, depending on him, and relating to him than he is in any external set of circumstances. So what about day three? The busted yolk was a success because you were drawn closer to your Father in the process. And that's no yolk.

Letting God get to say allows us to be free to try all sorts of new things, because the weight of the risk lies with him. Say it with me now: "God gets to say! God gets to say!" ⚠

Frankly, just pitching trust to you is hard. I like being queen of my own me-dom, no matter how inadequate or deadly I am as a ruler. I try to act like I want Jesus to "take my all," but deep down I really want him to take only some—and I want to say which bits.

Please remember: I'm not describing only people who are clinically depressed, phobicly fearful, or dangerously angry. Holding on to non-trust works just as well (sometimes better) for those in the vanilla-flavored stress/fear level.

STRESS FREE QUIZ ━━━━━━━━━━━━━━━━━━━━━━━

Another Inspirational and Self-Reflective Quiz

I saw a bumper sticker that read, "Reality is a crutch for people who can't handle science fiction." Hopefully, this quiz can help you get real.

1. Am I thoroughly satisfied with my behavior? (Hint: If you are reading this, your answer is no.) ___ Yes ___ No

2. If you answered no, write on the blank (or write in your notebook) what particular behavior you are least satisfied with. Potential examples: A) I'm scared to let my kids go to public school. B) I see the negative in most things my husband says. C) I hate clowns, so I won't take my children to the circus even though they are begging to go.

3. What are some knee-jerk reasons why you have this behavior? Examples: A) I'm afraid something bad will happen to my kids there. B) Historically, my husband offends people or says obnoxious things to me or otherwise writes checks that his body can't pay, and I then have to be the "forgiving adult" or bail him out. C) Clowns remind me of my childhood in Paris, which was traumatic.

---

4. What reflections does this reasoning unearth about your view of God or your view of yourself? (We're looking for potential lies. Ask a friend to help you.) Examples: A) I don't think God will protect my kids. B) I feel like God doesn't watch out for me, so I have to protect myself even with my spouse. C) While in Paris, my family was pounced upon by some religious people dressed as mimes. They followed us and made us guess all of their rules, which they pantomimed poorly. I feel it was unkind of God to create someone who would be a mime. Therefore, God does not seem to like us very much!

---

5. What statement sums up your view of God or yourself? (Ask God to help you.) Examples: A) I don't trust God. B) I don't trust God. C) I don't trust God.

---

6. Is there another lie hidden behind the first one? Examples: A) God isn't trustworthy. B) God isn't trustworthy. C) God isn't trustworthy.

THE SAFE ZONE

The final perk a lack of trust offers is that, like other forms of medication, it seemingly gives relief, although in a perverted, sick way. Remember, anything we use to lick our wounds and avoid going to God for rescue is medication, an idol, or—dare I say it?—a sin. Lack of trust is the ultimate med. By engaging in medicating, controlling, freaking out, withdrawing, or another non-trusting behavior, we scratch an itch, as it were, instead of dealing with the pus-surrounded splinter that is the true cause of the discomfort. It's putting a bandage over a gangrenous leg—it feels a little better because we've "treated it," and it allows us not to have to think of it for a while, which makes life seem manageable.

> Tomorrow is often the busiest day of the week.
> —SPANISH PROVERB

This area that we spend so much energy and effort on maintaining and protecting is known as our comfort zone. And the un-faith-filled what-ifs are incredibly useful in building and maintaining this zone. Think about it. Don't most what-ifs prevent (or protect) us from doing something new and different? How wonderful is *that*! Something comes up that's a little on the edge, a little zone-stretching? No problem, you can what-if that adventure right into terror-trauma oblivion. An invitation beckons you to do something you've never done before? What-if that thing right off the calendar.

Comfort zones either grow or shrink; they won't stay the same. The experts back me on this; they said it first. So if you aren't doing something daily to stretch your zone, it'll shrink like that expensive silk dress that said Dry Clean Only but ended up in the washer by mistake. And the more it shrinks, a comfort zone—unlike my waistline—is harder to stretch.

There are times when I will do anything to get rid of the perceived pain and stress *except* go to God. Why? Because I'm insane. You are too, I bet. And you know how Albert Einstein defined *insanity*: "doing the same thing over and over and expecting different results." (Yes, he really said it.)

Ultimately, we just can't imagine doing things differently. *What if I fail?* We don't feel we have the strength to try something new or to break the mold. *What if it's another tanker?* We don't have the courage. *What if God doesn't help me?* We don't have the trust. *What if trying to get better hurts more than I can bear?* Arthur Somers Roche pinpointed what's happening: "Worry is a thin stream of fear trickling through the mind. If encouraged, it cuts a channel into which all other thoughts are drained."

Believing the lies and hanging on to the fear, depression, guilt, and anger help our world stay small and familiar. Growth might hurt. Growth is uncertain. And the bottom line with growth is that we don't feel in control (not that we're ever really in control anyway).

> No pain, no gain!
> —SEEN ON EVERY WEIGHT-LIFTING WALL IN AMERICA

There are a plethora of reasons—payoffs, we call them—for non-trust. But what are the costs? Let me ask you, in what you've observed in your world on a day-to-day basis, what would be the price of not trusting God?

Well, what would happen if your young son refused to trust you? He would be afraid to hold your hand because you might lead him somewhere unsafe or to a place he didn't want to go. He wouldn't go down the slide because he was afraid you wouldn't catch him. He'd have trouble going to sleep because he wasn't sure you'd protect him. He'd refuse to hug you because he was afraid you might drop him.

How many things could you do with your son? How close could you get to him? What kind of relationship would you have? How would you feel as a parent?

Are these your answers? Not many. Not too close. Distant. Lonely, shallow, frustrated, sad, alienated, sad, helpless, sad . . .

What would you desperately wish you could do together? Why?

You'd want to show him that you can be trusted—so that he could enjoy life more and enjoy your time together. He's missing out on so much, and it's such a shame. If only he could see that things could be different . . . better. Just trusting you a little bit might change everything. Certainly there would be a few spills, some disappointments, some skinned knees . . . but the laughter and the experience and the intimacy that you two could enjoy together would so outweigh all the bad. If only . . .

Hmm. Maybe your heavenly Father feels the same way about you.

TAKE YOUR MEDS

You've seen those billboards that are supposed to be messages from God? I saw one that said, "I love you . . . I love you . . . I love you." Keep that in mind as you savor the message in Romans 15:13:

"May the God of hope fill you with all joy and peace as you trust in him, so that you may overflow with hope by the power of the Holy Spirit." ◼▶

1. Grab your notebook and record one thought about this chapter, one positive thing that happened today, one Scripture that you like, and one way that God has blessed you.

2. What struck you as interesting or unusual in this chapter? Why?

3. Choose one Scripture that you will try to memorize. Write it down.

4. Do you feel you've been taught well to trust God? If so, where, how, and from whom did you learn? If not, what *were* you taught about trusting God?

5. What do you think about the idea "God gets to say" as illustrated in "Frying Eggs with God" on page 133? Is there an area of your life in which you have more say than the Almighty does? Can you discuss that with a friend or your small group?

6. With a friend or small group, brainstorm some of the seeming benefits of non-trust. Did this chapter cover them all?

7. Brainstorm some of the costs of non-trust. Did you think of some not mentioned in this chapter?

7

BEATiNG iT SPIRiTUALLY

Success isn't permanent and failure isn't fatal.

—Mike Ditka

T
o beat any negative emotion, one must be willing to wage war. You must squeeze that enemy! Give him no mercy. As was said in the intellectually stimulating film *Big Fat Liar*, "I want you to turn [the enemy] into mincemeat, and I don't even know what mincemeat is! I want him to cry for his mommy! Wah! Wah! Mommy, Mommy, Mommy!"

This plan of attack will be split into three chapters because three is, according to Schoolhouse Rock, "a magic number, yes it is." These three components shalt henceforth be known as the spiritual, the emotional, and the physical levels. This is how we telleth the brain to be serious—by using Elizabethan-era words like *henceforth, thou, yore,* and *skimble-skamble* (an actual term meaning "rambling, disjointed") . . . or we can randomly add *eth* to words.

How does one spiritually attack fear? Well, with the Spirit, of course! We'll use an old-fashioned method in which you gather the forthcoming valuable instructions by actually reading through the chapter, thus preventing wanton skipping around from idea to idea all . . . skimble-skamble-eth. OK, remember those lies we discussed way back in chapter 4? Drag those sorry things out; we're going to deal with them posthaste.

> It is hard to fight an enemy who has outposts in your head.
>
> —SALLY KEMPTON

Let's say the lie you believe is that God won't take care of you. Perhaps you feel you're not worthy or that he's too busy or uninterested. You feel this way because when you pray, nothing seems to happen or the answers appear to be the opposite of what you ask. When struggles come (which they often do), God apparently has his back turned or is far away drinking Cosmic Dr Peppers on a Caribbean-style vacation in some other, less whiny, solar system.

At least that's how *I* felt. And though it amazes me now, there was nothing that could dissuade me—no clever logic, no urgent pleas, no sweet gifts from God, and no scolding from Chico Marx: "Who you gonna believe, me or your own eyes?" I had made my case against the Almighty, strapped on those condemnation goggles (whatever color those might be—brown, perchance?), draped the dreary wet blanket of negativity over my shoulders, and sharpened my pencil of cynicism so all things, good or bad, could be dutifully noted and filed in the See? God Doesn't Care for Me folder.

With great effort I managed to mangle various blessings from

God, forcing them (with the use of blind, stubborn, self-loathing will) through my God-doesn't-care filter. Yep, that was me—a blessing mangler. My favorite way to dismiss any gift from Jehovah: *Well, at least he likes Kevin and Meghan.* Or, *Yeah, but he didn't . . .* Or, *That was unusual . . . and lucky.* The Blessing Mangler strikes again! *Zip! Zap!*

My pain had seemingly become so huge, and I had swallowed (and wallowed in) the yonder aforementioned lie for so long, that I was utterly sincere in my complaint. The Old Testament character of Job was my hero because at least he stood up for himself when he had the chance. It never really crossed my synapses that my grudge was against the Almighty, the Creator, the omnipotent one, the überkahuna as it were.

And understand, I was still a believer and felt I was saved (mostly). But I was a disgruntled employee, a jilted lover, a pouty spiritual preteen who thought her Dad was a little slow on the uptake or, more specifically, at work all the time and never home or available for *me.* I had swallowed the enemy's poison hook, line, and sinker. I had bought it and made it mine.

It's almost funny, looking back. (Yeah, funny in a *Wow! I'm glad I didn't get roasted with a well-placed lightning bolt* sort of way.)

ADMIT THE PROBLEM

So the very first step to whipping the enemy's hinder region is to see where he's fed you a jug of moonshine. What is that lie you've sucked in?

And then you have to admit you have a problem. Duh. Say it with me: "I have a problem. Duh." There. Doesn't that feel better?

Confessed faults are half-mended.

—SCOTTISH PROVERB

Seriously. We often do everything possible not to admit it. "My husband is a controlling jerk—that's why I'm angry." "I've had horrible things happen in my past—that's why I don't trust anyone." "The world is a frightening place—that's why I'm stressed out and afraid."

Stop. Go back. Please know I'm deeply sorry that you've had some bad things and people negatively affect your life. Even so, if you are using any event or person as an excuse for why you do or don't do things, especially on a consistent basis, return to chapter 4, reread it, and see if you can find what lie you believe about yourself and God.

The bottom line is, you have to admit (it used to be called confessing) that you don't trust God. Otherwise, the fear, anger, and other negative attitudes and behaviors will remain. Can you admit that now, or will you (like me) have to go back around the mountain again and again and again?

First, admit to yourself, *I have a problem trusting God.* Or, *I don't think I'm worthy of being loved by God.* Or, *It feels hopeless.* Or, *I feel like I'll never get better—I'm hopeless.*

Then you need to admit it to God. Of course, he already knows about you and your shortcomings in toto (um . . . no, not *The Wizard of Oz* dog). But it's good to say it out loud and as often as you realize it's happening. Here's how I started: "Lord, I'm very sorry that I don't trust you. I'd like to do it better—at least I think I would—but I'm not sure I can. Please help me." OK, so you don't have to sound as confident, but the goal is simply to tell God what he's known all along and to apologize for believing the lie.

Your admission can be offered in any fashion that your heart desires: you can pray your apology, write it down, sing about it, paint it, or dance it—whatever works best for you. Take time to tell God you realize you've been dancing with the wrong partner (that's Texas-speak for "messed up"). And ask him to forgive you.

I also had to ask God to forgive me for having a bundle of expectations for him to meet. Ashleigh Brilliant said, "All I want is a warm bed and a kind word and unlimited power."

Without realizing it, I had compiled quite a script for the maker of all things to follow: "Let's see, three well-adjusted, high-achieving, non-embarrassing children; a personally thin but healthy body (a constant 130 pounds, please, regardless of what I put in my pie hole); naturally blonde hair; to be a stay-at-home/homeschool mom (award-winning of course) with a cool, profitable side career (award-winning of course); a soulmate husband who worships the ground I walk on; a nice house with a beautiful garden (effortless and award-winning); and oh yeah, constant happiness. And no disappointments. Ever. Yeah thanks, God. That'll do for now. Amen."

SOOTHING INTROSPECTION

Searching Questions

Do you have a script for God to fill for your life?
What does your script look like? (Write it out, if possible.)
How's he doing at following it?

Unfortunately (or fortunately, depending on your perspective), following my script—contrary to what I think or what is preached on the health/wealth channels—is not what God was made for, lives for, or longs to spend his time doing. I'm not the first or only one who has wrestled with this, nor is "scripting" God the only dumb thing we try with Jehovah. You may have your own special particulars that need to be confessed and repented of. God will show you.

It's like going to the doctor with a broken leg you keep hitting with a hammer. Doc assesses the injury and wants to put the leg in a cast. Instead, you say, "No thanks, I'm doing fine. I just wanted to know why my leg looked funny and hurt so much." And you crawl away, smacking yourself some more with the hammer. Dumb analogy, but we are about as brilliant in dealing with our unbelief or lies that separate us from God. Even after we realize what's happening, we carry on—for whatever set of imbecilic reasons—crippling ourselves as we go.

> To the man who only has a hammer in the toolkit, every problem looks like a nail.
>
> —ABRAHAM MASLOW

My Catholic friends understand the spiritual value of confessing, considering it a natural part of forgiveness. Confession cleanses. Going to a priest for forgiveness of sin is not the ticket, but telling someone you trust helps to break the wall of silence and shame. In that moment another person knows something deep, and presumably dark, about you and is willing to pray for you and still care about you. Confessing to God opens the door to healing and absolution; God promises to release your error through Jesus (Hebrews 7:24-26; 1 John 1:9).

> Once we accept our limits, we go beyond them.
>
> —ALBERT EINSTEIN

Picture a child fessing up to something. At first the little punk is overwhelmed with guilt. His whole body seems under a massive weight, and his feet drag heavily as he moves toward the place of death—the place where he must confess what he did. But once the admission is complete, a dramatic transformation occurs: there's a brightness in his face and a spring in his step; he almost bounces as he bounds down the street, exonerated and released from the bondage of guilt and shame.

THE BENEFITS OF CONFESSION

Confession does the same for us (oh, to bound down the street again!) by loosening the grip of guilt as we pull the secret black thing from our hearts and out into the light. The enemy then loses power because he works best in dark, dank, secret places like New Jersey. No! I mean the dark, secret places of our minds and hearts. (New Jersey is a *lovely* place—I only chose it so often because I don't think I know anyone there. If you're offended, please know I didn't mean it, and I can change the dark place to Buffalo.) Confession pops that satanic pimple as it were, acting like spiritual Clearasil, cleansing it and allowing it to heal.

A secondary benefit of confession is that we often get assistance—not only from the Holy Spirit but also from those who know we are struggling. Prayers, even when we're unaware they're being offered, aid us in a mysterious, supernatural way that I don't really understand. "The earnest prayer of a righteous person has great power and wonderful results" (James 5:16, *NLT*). It's *big*. It's unchartable. It's where the Creator does things in dimensions and ways our created brains can't grasp without exploding. Therefore, I'm not going to talk about them.

TAKE YOUR MEDS

Meditate on Psalm 79:9:

"Help us, O God our Savior, for the glory of your name; deliver us and forgive our sins for your name's sake."

Look up the Lord's Prayer in your Bible (Matthew 6:9-13) and pray it.

Read Psalm 103:2-5:

"Praise the LORD, O my soul, and forget not all his benefits—who forgives all your sins and heals all your diseases, who redeems your life from the pit and crowns you with love and compassion, who satisfies your desires with good things so that your youth is renewed like the eagle's."

Read 1 John 1:9 and do it:

"If we confess our sins, he is faithful and just and will forgive us our sins and purify us from all unrighteousness." ◼▶

The Bible is pretty emphatic about the importance of confession. We should "confess [our] sins to each other and pray for each other so that [we] may be healed" (James 5:16). But I don't want to do it.

Yeah, I know James was the brother of Jesus, so he probably had some good things to say. But frankly, I don't want people to see that I'm even worse deep down than I might seem on the surface. Yet regardless of how I *feel*, confession works because God made it that way.

I found this out accidentally. After writing about the struggle with fear in the *BryanPost* (our personal ministry newsletter with the motto: Cleverly Whining Since 1994), I was stunned by the positive and empathetic response. This helped me. It made me realize that many of my friends were as sick as I was! It also provided a network of people who offered to pray for me when a trip or other fear-inducing activity came up. These prayers, I think, ultimately gave me the fortitude to continue to face the fears and fight the demons.

> I don't understand you. You don't understand me. What else do we have in common?
>
> —ASHLEIGH BRILLIANT

You'd think I would like confessing because I like talking. I even find help in sharing struggles; I generally make more sense of a problem by just talking it out. Letting the junk flow from my brain and out of my mouth puts things into perspective. Emotions are released and make the conundrum seem not so huge. Thoughts and attitudes are better evaluated, often revealing that I'm holding on to fears or negative thoughts or toxic feelings.

Of course, then I change the subject and try to dig up some dirt on the one who is listening. No need to get too cleaned out!

But all this yapping *must* lead to something positive. James connects confession to prayer. In the Garden of Gethsemane, a sinless Jesus (not that Jesus actually yapped) voiced his fear and then ultimately obeyed the Father. Paul was led to go, preach, or write stressful letters. My praying, confessing, or constructive yapping needs to lead to some Spirit-guided action in order for me to grow and heal. It might be asking for prayer. Many times it's making a simple plan. Occasionally, it's waiting on the Lord, confronting someone, forgiving a person from the heart, or something equally irritating. So as good as confession is, if it doesn't lead to some sort of positive motion (and even waiting can be action, if you're waiting on the Lord), it quickly degenerates into whining, complaining, and gossiping.

The proverb says, "Confession is good for the soul." So find someone safe with whom you can share your struggles. If you don't have anyone, ask God to bring that person to you.

CHOOSE TO BELIEVE GOD

Once the lie is identified and confessed as sin, we then have to see what God says. In my case it was about this topic of Not Caring for Marcy. So what *does* God say about this particular pit-message? (Any more, I really *want* to move forward. If I stay in distress mode, my family will encouragingly say, "You want some cheese with that whine, or you just want a glass?")

"'I know the plans I have for you,' declares the LORD, 'plans to prosper you and not to harm you, plans to give you hope and a future'" (Jeremiah 29:11). Interestingly, God spoke this directly to the Israelites through the prophet Jeremiah just before they were carted off into exile and immediately after their towns and temple had been reduced to smoldering charcoal . . . AND the eyes of their king had been poked out by the captors. Even so, it seems to me that this promise from Yahweh can easily apply to all of God's people through Christ regardless of their circumstances. Therefore, you'd think he could still have a few good plans left, even for me.

"Never will I leave you [*meaning those who believe in him*]; never will I forsake you [*meaning leave you vulnerable and uncared for*]" (Hebrews 13:5). Let us implant this deeper than our pores and into our souls. If you are a Christian who believes in Jesus, this verse applies to you and means what it says. I, for one, still need reminding.

"Which of you fathers, if your son asks for a fish, will give him a snake instead? Or if he asks for an egg, will give him a scorpion? If you then, though you are evil, know how to give good gifts to your children, how much more will your Father in heaven give the Holy Spirit to those who ask him!" (Luke 11:11-13). Again, Jesus is teaching to a specific audience, but it would seem that this assemblage included potential followers.

This means us. God wants to place within us a part of himself—the Holy Spirit, who connects us to our Father in a special and intimate way. If that isn't happening, then it may be because we haven't asked, we aren't letting the Holy Spirit do what he wants to do, we aren't hearing his call because we've tuned our antennas to another source . . . or all of the above. Or it may simply be a desert time, one of those strange moments during which life unaccountably stinks—things around you seem to be going along OK, but you feel dry and lifeless inside.

When God feels distant, search and pray to see whether there is something obstructing you and God. (This author at times had to deal with all of the above, and then some. I won't tell you what or how much; it's too embarrassing.) If you can't discover the obstruction, then hold on to Hebrews 13:5 and keep praying.

TAKE YOUR MEDS

Enjoy this passage from Matthew 6:27-34 in *The Message*:

"Has anyone by fussing in front of the mirror ever gotten taller by so much as an inch? All this time and money wasted on fashion—do you think it makes that much difference? Instead of looking at the fashions, walk out into the fields and look at the wildflowers. They never primp or shop, but have you ever seen color and design quite like it? . . . If God gives such attention to the appearance of wildflowers—most of which are never even seen—don't you think he'll attend to you, take pride in you, do his best for you? . . . Give your entire attention to what God is doing right now, and don't get worked up about what may or may not happen tomorrow. God will help you deal with whatever hard things come up when the time comes."

There are many other verses, but these will do. As a follower of Jesus, there comes a time when I have to choose (no matter what my emotions *scream*) to believe either what the Scriptures say or what *I* say because, let's face it, they are often mutually exclusive. I can't believe that God doesn't take care of me and at the same time believe God's Word that says, "Never will I leave you" and "You are worth more than . . ."

So we're back to choosing. Or starting to choose. Or praying about choosing. Remember, choosing requires no overt feeling necessarily; nor does it require any immediate observable action—all the stinking work might stay deep in the unseen areas for a long time. But staying in the lie definitely means remaining in the fear, depression, and the rest of the junk. If you feel like you can hardly choose the truth, ask God to help you. I had to. And there are days when I continue to have to. (But keep that on the QT, will you please? I'm trying to look like an expert.)

Unfortunately, as you come against those past years of falsehood, you will *feel* very uncomfortable, especially at first. You are not a hypocrite at these moments, although the accuser will offer some persuasive arguments to the contrary. You are in the process of conforming your mind to Christ's. If, for instance, you've ever used a wrong technique to hold a golf club, a bat, or a snow cone, you know how awkward it is when you try to change your grip to the correct one. The better position seems totally wrong until the erring reflexes are retrained.

> Heaven goes by favor; if it went by merit, you would stay out and your dog would go in.
>
> —MARK TWAIN

A more difficult (and longer) question is not "Are you *trying* to choose truth?" but "Are you *saying* you choose truth but are, fundamentally, *behaving* as though you believe (and are therefore actually agreeing with) the lie?"

Kevin wanted to take our daughter on a surprise trip. San Francisco became the target vacation destination. As we checked out the amenities of the Bay region, Kev noticed they could kayak by the Golden Gate Bridge. My immediate response: "You can't take Meghan kayaking! . . . Why? This past spring two young people died in kayak accidents." My mind instantly claimed the what-if-Meghan-dies-kayaking lie as truth. I agreed with it and reacted. I *say* I trust God (and Kevin) with my daughter. (Notice she's *my* daughter here. Meghan generally becomes *his* daughter when she needs discipline or money.) But I act as if I'm the only one with brains enough to keep her safe.

> One of the symptoms of an approaching nervous breakdown is the belief that one's work is terribly important.
>
> —BERTRAND RUSSELL

No matter where you are in this choice continuum, know that your Father loves you. Choosing to live in the lie certainly affects your relationship with him and prevents you from doing some cool things through the power of the Holy Spirit. But it doesn't mean that you aren't going to Heaven. If you have accepted Jesus as your Savior, then you're in the family. You may be a self-made spiritual paraplegic, duct-taped to chains and anchors, gnawing off your own arms; but you're still family. By the way, I'll probably be the one sitting next to you—with the royal blue duct tape all over me. Silver clashes with my eyes.

This confessing and choosing is hard work. Here are a few other tools that might come in handy.

GIVE YOURSELF GRACE

The grace of God not only makes excellent ammo with which to blow away those heinous and deadly lies, it also makes Christianity both the most attractive and distressing belief system imaginable. Allowing God to get to say how we (and other people) are doing in this life is incredibly freeing, but unbelievably vexing because, let's face it, we like to control things.

God's grace is irksome in that it makes your relationship with your Father a personal experience that no one completely understands. It's like a bunch of college kids living together in a frat house: the newbie adults love it and often become best friends forever, stuff gets done . . . But the place looks like a toxic waste heap, and everyone over thirty considers it an unsafe, chaotic, brain-cell-deadening pit that should be condemned and immediately torn down. What's true? Does looking like a waste heap make it so? Why must we value only that which lies upon the surface? Since when does learning exclusively occur in the sterile, vacuous halls of public education? (Feel free to find a college person and tell him what you think about this. Use words like *gnarly, bogus, groovy,* and *hip* to get his attention and connect with him. He'll appreciate it.)

I think of grace as my favorite chair on a deck by the beach. Grace feels like a summer day with butterflies, flowers, and a light breeze. Of course, grace includes a back rub and some nice chocolate. And maybe a long, hot bath. Grace especially includes an understanding that God loves you where you are. It's also realizing that where you are at this moment isn't where you will stay—today doesn't equal forever. It's taking (and holding on to) the view that each day, month, and year you are in a different place. If you are trying to face your fears, capture your thoughts, and trust Jesus—no matter how slightly—you cannot remain in the same spot; you are growing and moving forward. You can be exceedingly grateful and supremely joyful for that.

> I do not at all understand the mystery of grace—only that it meets us where we are but does not leave us where it found us.
>
> —ANNE LAMOTT

If we are ruled by grace, does that prevent us from getting better? No. It's just that grace will 1) make the effort, and the journey, more hope-filled and joyful; and 2) alter the motivation of our attempts to change. With grace, being correct is not as important as being cherished. Since we are already adored by the only one who truly matters, healing becomes an expression and a result of being loved by, and in love with, him—and not simply a method by which we keep our "sorry carcasses" out of Hell. It's not just a difference of semantics; it's a difference of perspective, which changes everything.

A component of grace essential to winning this war is—this is profound, so read it slowly and dramatically—ta-da! Acceptance.

I can vividly recall (cue dramatic flashback music) when this started for me: (Fade in.) One day after Bible study, I was driving home and trying to pray. When I'm struggling with crud in my life, prayer either sounds like a whiny pity party or nothing at all. I was in the nothing-at-all stage. "Dear God . . . (silence) . . . (a Charlie-Brown-type heavy *sigh*)."

On this particular day I made a monstrous step—"Dear God, it's just me, Marcy [in case God might not know who it is. You know he's pretty busy and has a lot of people to deal with and] . . . (silence) . . . *Sigh*." After a while I graduated to—"Dear God, it's just me, Marcy. (Tears start to fall.) Help me . . . (silence) . . . *Sigh*." No excuses, no bargaining, no nothing. Just me showing my naked self to Yahweh. Willingly.

In time, the "just me" part moved from meaning "a whiny, pathetic, miserable, ungrateful loser" to "a whiny, pathetic, miserable, *grateful* loser who is unique and whom God bought and loves anyway. *Sigh*." That subtle change was stunning—I still was neck deep in the lies that dominated my mind, but I had grasped a few microns of truth: I was God's and he loved me (or at least didn't hate me), no matter what I looked like or did. And I could, in fact, *be aware of it and be thankful.* Yee-haw! Progress!

⚠ FRIGHTENING STUFF

Some What-Is Statements for Your Consideration

Eugene O'Neill said, "Man is born broken. He lives by mending. The grace of God is glue." Feel free to tack these statements to your mirror, refrigerator, microwave oven, your own forehead, or the foreheads of your children and coworkers.

God will never leave me or abandon me. (from Hebrew 13:5)

God loved me before I loved him. (from 1 John 4:19)

Jesus loves me, this I know, for the Bible tells me so. (from a children's song and John 13:1)

There is nothing I can do that can make God love me more, or less, than he does right now. (from Ephesians 2 and John 10:27, 28) ⚠

Before you write me angry letters of the "I can't believe she'd promote that wacko humanistic philosophy" sort, you're right—there is a type of self-acceptance that is very dangerous and ungodly. Here's why: Often we think self-acceptance means to love ourselves and believe that we *deserve* healing or happiness or a perfect body, spouse, or life. This isn't biblical or healthy. The apostle Paul says, "Do not think of yourself more highly than you ought, but rather think of yourself with sober judgment, in accordance with the measure of faith God has given you" (Romans 12:3).

Yet the Bible also says, "Love your neighbor as yourself"—ten times: twice in the Old Testament and eight times in the New (Leviticus 19:18 and Matthew 19:19, for example). So there must be some way to love ourselves yet not think too highly of ourselves. Eugene Peterson proposes a potential solution with his interpretation of Romans 12:3 in The Message: "The only accurate way to understand ourselves is by what God is and by what he does for us, not by what we are and what we do for him."

Over the years, deep disappointment has plagued me because I felt that God, Kevin, Meghan, my extended family, and yea verily, the population of my home state of Nebraska (motto: Cows outnumber people, so watch your step!) should somehow obey and honor me because of what I've done for them! *Look! How I cook and clean! And take care of my family's needs! No one else sacrifices like this! And I try to serve God well! And be good! And I do stuff I don't even like, for the sake of serving others! God ought to be very pleased!* (See how subtly we enter the wouldacouldashoulda zone, even with God?) *Kneel before me in honor and amazement!*

News flash: This is not godly self-acceptance. It's self-indulgence. And sin.

But if I honestly take time to look at Romans 12:3 and contemplate my life and what God has really done for me, I cry—not because I'm disappointed but because I can hardly believe how kind God has been.

I have friends who have gone through, or who are going through, unbelievably horrible struggles and losses. They are totally overwhelmed—not by their circumstance but by God's kindness and love. I honestly don't understand how they handle their trials, and often neither do they. But they're aware that God amazingly seems to show up at whatever level they need or allow him.

STRESS FREE QUIZ

Wouldacouldashoulda

Do you wouldacouldashoulda God? Check all that apply.

____ The martyr syndrome: *I've given up so much, even (fill in the blank), so you'd think God would . . .*

____ The Santa Claus syndrome: *I've been a good boy/girl, so God should . . .*

____ The Avis rental car syndrome: *I've tried harder, so God ought to . . .*

_____ The Rip Van Winkle syndrome: *I've been at this for so long, you'd think God would . . .*

_____ The reverse psychology on the Almighty syndrome: *If you're so big, God, why don't you just . . . ?*

Each of the above syndromes has *I* as the subject, the main thing, the big cheese. This happens to be the total opposite of the facts found in Romans 12:3.

I'm still working on accepting myself as God accepts me, seeing myself as he sees me *right now*: a precious child (John 1:12, 13); something valuable that he spent a fortune (i.e., the life of his Son) to purchase (Ephesians 5:1, 2); a saint who is more amazing than the mighty angels even though she still sins (Romans 8:27; Hebrews 1:14); a beautiful bride (Revelation 19:6-8). OK, the Scriptures don't describe individual Christians as brides. That term is reserved for the collective group of all Christians, known as the church. So if you want to be technical, you aren't a beautiful bride; you are a *piece* of a beautiful bride. I think I shall be the left upper lip. Pick your body part!

There is a famous statement credited to several people, including a friend of Rich Mullins's named Dave Busby, Reverend Desmond Tutu, and liberal theologian Virginia Mollenkott. It says, "Grace means there is nothing I can do to make God love me more, and nothing I can do to make God love me less."[1] I've also heard it worded, "There is nothing you can do that can make God love you more, or less, than he does right now." Writer/minister Brennan Manning said it this way: "God loves us as we are, not as we should be, for we will never be as we should be."[2] Look at those quotes again. The healthy focus is not on what I have or haven't done; it's all about God and what *he* has done (loved me) and hasn't done (left me). Accepting that is crucial for the blossoming of grace.

ACCEPT LOVE

The largest and most powerful tool on the workbench of healing is love. And love, by the way, is something that those of us who struggle with fear can't seem to accept—not from God or anyone else. It goes straight back to those stinking lies. Check your love-acceptance level the next time someone gives you a friendly hug. Really be aware of how you accept it. If you struggle with giving or, especially, getting hugs—even by an internal cringing or resistance of any kind—it's time to pray and ask God what's going on.

> Never forget that the most powerful force on earth is love.
>
> —NELSON ROCKEFELLER

Really accepting love from God might feel weird, but it's vital to overcoming fears, worries, and what-ifs. I thought I wanted God's love, and I did—I was dying to get it—but when good things happened or if I had to admit that he loved me in specific ways, there were usually yeah-buts. You know those yeah-buts—"Do you know that God loves you?" *Yeah, but I didn't get that promotion.* "Isn't it cool that God gave you such a great daughter?" *Yeah, but I wanted another baby so she wouldn't have to grow up alone.*

Yeah-buts totally negate the good that God has done for you. It's like taking a huge Sharpie and scratching out the positive event. And many Christians yeah-but God all the time, rejecting his blessings and spitting on his kindness—and sometimes call it, stunningly, humility. Check yourself out. In order to begin accepting God's love, you must stop yeah-butting him. Instead, gratefully accept God's kindness, love, and grace as they break through into your awareness. He really does love you. Really.

TAKE YOUR MEDS

Ephesians 3:16-21:

"I pray that out of his glorious riches he may strengthen you with power through his Spirit in your inner being, so that Christ may dwell in your hearts through faith. And I pray that you, being rooted and established in love, may have power, together with all the saints, to grasp how wide and long and high and deep is the love of Christ, and to know this love that surpasses knowledge—that you may be filled to the measure of all the fullness of God. Now to him who is able to do immeasurably more than all we ask or imagine, according to his power that is at work within us, to him be glory in the church and in Christ Jesus throughout all generations, for ever and ever! Amen." 💊

PRAY AND WAIT

In regard to the possibility of being totally, instantly, and miraculously healed, all I can say is, go ahead and pray for an immediate, supernatural cure, but know it doesn't always happen that way.

> If it's free, it's advice; if you pay for it, it's counseling; if you can use either one, it's a miracle.
>
> —JACK ADAMS

Sometimes God uses struggles in order to accomplish better things. Take Paul's "thorn in [the] flesh" (2 Corinthians 12:7); it was generously dished out to him (apparently from Satan) so he wouldn't get the big head over all the understanding, special insight, visions, and people God had given him. Even though Paul prayed diligently for healing, God never acquiesced but said instead, "My grace is sufficient for you, for my power is made perfect in weakness" (v. 9).

I'm not saying that you have to live with debilitating fear, depression, or anger forever. What I am saying is that we may end up struggling in certain areas while we are here on earth. And because I'm a sensitive, enlightened, co-struggling writer, I've made up some insightful and logical reasons why we're not always cured instantly:

1. There may be lessons to learn that you couldn't get any other way, as illustrated in the famous Nietzsche quote, "That which does not kill us makes us stronger."

2. You can offer more comfort and grace after you've suffered or struggled. Remember: "Carry each other's burdens, and in this way you will fulfill the law of Christ" (Galatians 6:2). That's why you see so many women who've had abortions helping at crisis pregnancy ministries. Former homosexuals are generally the ones who have the best outreach to the gay community.

3. Non-Christians watch how you handle tough times because that's when a person's true colors are revealed. As they watch the grace of God and the love of his people at work, their lives can be touched for eternity.

4. Other Christians watch too. Those who are presently in the thick, as it were, identify and find hope by observing and walking alongside those who have gone before and who are making progress.

SOW AND REAP

A final skill you'll need to cultivate is atomic engineering. Just kidding! Atomic engineering will not help you in the least. What you *really* need is an understanding about sowing and reaping. Galatians 6:7 makes it plain: "Do not be deceived: God cannot be mocked. A man reaps what he sows."

In gardening, the desired outcome (harvesting) drives each step of the process. In the beginning is the cultivation plan where seed catalogs reach near-Holy-Writ status; garden centers become Mecca; and an elusive cutting, nirvana. Seeds, identified as cute little teddy bear sunflowers, stunning daffodils, and smelly (in a good way) herbs like lavender, rosemary, and basil are finally chosen, purchased, and planted (after the gardener has been assured that spring has actually sprung). Then the entire bed receives mulch and fertilizer and much TLC.

Amongst all of the gardener's duties, being wishful is the most obvious because he or she diligently hopes to grow plants and prevent the inevitable weeds from invading their precious beds—all with as little effort as possible. Unfortunately, plants are weenies that must be babied, and weeds are sneaky but hardy miscreants that must be searched out and eradicated with a fervor that has been seen only among monkeys grooming each other and during the McCarthy "There's a Communist in our midst" era.

There are other tasks as well. On any given day (and until the gardener finally gives up and just paves the spot), he finds himself weeding, watering, weeding, fertilizing, weeding, watering, weeding, and replanting. And waiting. There's a great deal of waiting. Yet the garden will perish and the weeds will win if any one of these steps is messed with.

Like a garden, the mind also needs to be continuously tended, or those hideous weeds of negativity and fear will win.

> If I had to live my life again, I'd make the same mistakes, only sooner.
> —TALLULAH BANKHEAD

Also keep in mind that *what* one plants is as important as how and when. If you plant carrots, you can't expect sunflowers; if you plant corn, you won't get daisies. This might seem glaringly obvious, but it's true with your thoughts as well. What you sow, you will reap. Plant negative, degrading thoughts; reap negative, degrading behavior. You can't plant what-ifs and harvest joy, because what-ifs are spiritual stinging nettles. And if that's what you've been planting, let's stop acting like you've put in hydrangeas. I had to fess up to it, so you might as well too. I hate being the only one!

Your Own Personal Time Line Activity

Gather one sheet of paper for every decade you have lived.

Turn each sheet sideways and write the decades at the tops.

Draw a line across the middle of each sheet.

Write on the lines any outstanding memories that you can think of (good or bad). Try to place the memories in the approximate spot on the lines when they happened during that decade.

After completing this, tape the sheets together to form one long time line.

Set it aside for a few hours (or days).

Come back to it. Add anything else you've thought of.

Now look over your time line for patterns and threads. I used a highlight marker to color-code things that seemed similar.

To get the most out of this, show it to someone you trust. Have some really good chocolate or dessert and a Starbucks or other favorite beverage, and share your time lines. It might feel silly at first; but as you go through them aloud, you will see all sorts of things you missed or special groupings of events. You'll have other insights. It will be very enlightening for both of you.

Take a moment and look at your life honestly. What have you sown into it? OK, let's not look at your *whole* life. Let's look at today. If you want to know what seeds you've planted in the past, just look at your life *now,* because you're reaping from past planting. What does your harvest look like? How do you react to things—especially the negative and unexpected? That's reaping. How do you handle disappointment or stress? What do you do when you are not OK? How do you treat your family when you feel icky? If you aren't doing the things you wish you were, could it be that you didn't plant the right seeds? Every thought is a seed. What you see and read and hear are seeds. The words that come out of your mouth can be seeds. For instance, do you put yourself down? You are sowing curses against your own self.

Are you planting fear into your life or the lives of your children and others close to you? Are you planting depression? What about anger? What's your harvest? Debt? Obesity? An eating disorder? Sleepless nights? Some type of addiction? Do you like what you've been reaping?

Whatever type of seeds you planted in your past, that's what you're harvesting now. So if you planted bad seeds, that's the bad news.

SOOTHING INTROSPECTION

Organic Introspection

If you were an agriculture specialist coming to analyze the harvest of your attitudes and behaviors, how would you grade the crop? What suggestions would you give for how the harvest could be different next season?

If you're *really* brave, do this with your kids. Take along a box of tissues. Kids are ruthless because they actually tell the truth.

Dave Barry said, "You can only be young once. But you can always be immature." That's funny, but we want to grow. The great news is that you can sow now to harvest better attitudes and behaviors in the near future. Seeds are amazing. One kernel off that corncob will produce a stalk taller than you, with three or four ears of hundreds of kernels each—and rather quickly too. Spiritually, you don't have to plant impressively huge things. Some of the seemingly smallest alterations can bring gargantuan results in your life. Changing the way you see God might not be visible to the naked eye, but the impact could be completely mind-blowing. Trusting God in a new way might make you feel naked and vulnerable, but the growth you'll experience is monstrous (in a good way).

One more thing: stop agreeing with the enemy. That's like planting poison ivy in your garden. When you find yourself thinking, *I'm such a loser, I'm an idiot,* and *This is hopeless . . .* no matter how true those may *feel,* counter them with, *I might* feel *like a loser. Thanks, God, for sending your Son to save all people, including me, no matter how they feel.* Or, *I may* feel *like an idiot. Thanks, Jesus, for coming down to my level and loving me where I am. Please help me see your truth beyond how I feel.*

The more you do this, the better able you will be to determine which seed is, in fact, a painful weed and then reject it. The more good seeds you plant, the more wonderful the harvest of God-stuff in your life will be.

To sum up: Beating fear on the spiritual level takes admission, confession, patience, and lots of other ammo in the form of various tools and skills.

TAKE YOUR MEDS

Consider Ephesians 2:4-10:

"Because of his great love for us, God, who is rich in mercy, made us alive with Christ even when we were dead in transgressions—it is by grace you have been saved. And God raised us up with Christ and seated us with him in the heavenly realms in Christ Jesus, in order that in the coming ages he might show the incomparable riches of his grace, expressed in his kindness to us in Christ Jesus. For it is by grace you have been saved,

through faith—and this not from yourselves, it is the gift of God—not by works, so that no one can boast. For we are God's workmanship, created in Christ Jesus to do good works, which God prepared in advance for us to do." ◖▶

1. Grab your notebook and record one thought about this chapter, one positive thing that happened today, one Scripture that you like, and one way that God has blessed you.

2. What struck you as interesting or unusual in this chapter? Why?

3. Choose one Scripture that you will try to memorize. Write it down.

4. What is one lie you've believed? With what Scripture truth can you replace that?

5. What one Scripture truth have you been *saying* you believed but not *behaving* as if you believed? How can you work on that?

6. Besides the suggestions in this chapter, can you think of other reasons why a person might not be instantly healed? How might God use your struggles for your own spiritual growth?

Remember to check the Resources section on page 247.

BEATiNG iT EMOTiONALLY

If you realized how powerful your thoughts are, you would never think a negative thought.

—MILDRED RYDER

W e're now moving into the second phase of healing, the emotional zone. As we beat these negative emotions, we have to get beyond our "feelers," because it is our feelers that cling to the what-ifs, if-onlys, and yeah-buts.

At times we don't even realize that a sequence of negativity and overwhelming thoughts is happening. For example, if I feel uncomfortable at a meeting or other gathering, I might initially describe it in my mind with reasonable thoughts like, *I don't like crowds* or, *I'm having a bad day* or, *I'm feeling overwhelmed because I have too much to do and don't want to be here. Meetings are useless anyway; nothing really gets done, which means they are time wasters and possibly from the devil.* (pouty face) *So why am I here?*

I may in fact be struggling with the fear of rejection. Without even realizing it, I may have mentally processed, *What if they don't like me?* or, *What if I don't know anyone and they all ignore me because I don't fit in?* I may have traveled from those thoughts to feeling defensive, rejected, outcast, and stressed out—with no awareness of the process that got me there.

When battling bad emotions, one of the most effective ways to beat them is to stop the cycle of negativity and overwhelming thoughts before it starts. The cycle often begins with the what-ifs and quickly deteriorates into thinking about the worst possible scenario in all its Technicolor gory . . . I mean glory.

The result of such vain imaginings is that your body responds as if the threat were real and imminent. Your heart rate changes, your breathing changes, your attitude certainly changes—usually becoming more defensive, and your demeanor changes to prepare for . . . (say it with feeling!) . . . fight or flight!

Try it yourself. Think of someone to whom you would like to tell something. It can be the president, your mother-in-law, your spouse, your father, a sibling, or an ex-friend. Choose a topic that has quite a bit of emotion in it; for example, talking to your mom (or mother-in-law) about how you are raising your kids. Perhaps you aren't doing it the way she prefers, but even so, you believe putting the children in clown school is the best choice for their future and your family. (As tempting as it might be to use this example, you must choose your own. That is why it is called an example, a Greek word meaning "I thought of it first, so you have to pick something else.")

Now, in your mind have that discussion. You know the arguments; you've heard them—blatantly or subtly—a thousand times, so it should be fairly easy to fantasize what the person would say to you and how it would be said. Go ahead. Say whatever you would like (keep it in your mind, please) in whatever manner you wish. Just let yourself go. I'll wait here.

I argue very well. Ask any of my remaining friends.

—DAVE BARRY

Let me know if you need some more time.

Remember, you can also imagine this about a boss or that insufferable lady at the service desk of a will-not-be-named major retail chain who didn't believe that you just had your receipt but now can't find it anywhere, so she gave you only half of what you spent on that overpriced dress because it magically went on clearance today.

Keep going a little bit longer.

Did you get it all out? Gave the person a powerful, yet proverbial, piece of your mind, did you? How do you feel? If you performed the way I had hoped, you'll feel exhausted. Or agitated. How's your heart rate? You'll find it has risen if you threw yourself into the scenario. How's your attitude? Want to go to dinner (or on vacation) with that person right now?

This ingenious exercise shows that your "thinker" (mind) and especially your "feeler" (emotions) can propel your "doer" (body) wherever they will. Strange, my thinker and feeler want my doer to have a cookie. I think Mark Twain was right: "A man's private thought can never be a lie; what he thinks, is to him the truth, always." So . . . um, I'll be right back because I. Must. Get. Cookie.

The ingenious exercise also illustrates the obvious motive for that bothersome passage in Philippians 4:8 where Paul encourages, "Finally, brothers, whatever is true, whatever is noble, whatever is right, whatever is pure, whatever is lovely, whatever is admirable—if anything is excellent or praiseworthy—think about such things." Thinking about good things instead of negative things forces our feeling parts to hup, two, three, four—which ultimately affects our doing parts. An extra benefit from good thinking is that positive (and especially biblical or godly) thoughts actually help renew the mind (Roman 12:2) and protect it (Philippians 4:7).

> A woman's mind is cleaner than a man's because she changes it more often.
> —ATTRIBUTED TO BOTH OLIVER HERFORD AND MARK TWAIN

When Bob Russell was my minister, I heard him reflect on which of the Lord's commandments was the hardest for him to obey. Some would have said that "Love your neighbor" or "Do not covet" or even "Be pure" might be the most difficult. But Bob said that the commandment "Do not let your hearts be troubled" (John 14:1) was the hardest for him to follow. He confessed that his faith and his heart could easily be "ground down" by the what-ifs because his biggest temptation was to worry. I'd certainly have to agree. That's the basis of this whole book.

BREAK THE CYCLE OF NEGATIVITY

One key way to break the mind and emotions of their naughty negative habits is to shock them out of the what-ifs as soon as they come up. And since you can't leave your mind empty (just try to think of nothing), you must remove those icky thoughts (*icky* is the proper psychological term) and replace them with the truth of God's what-is statements. Paul said as much, but used fewer words, in 2 Corinthians 10:5: "We take captive every thought to make it obedient to Christ." Sounds good, right? But is it really possible?

Let's become aware of our thought processes, shall we? Many experts (meaning me, myself, and I) recommend the rubber-band-on-the-wrist method. Meghan picked this up from our friend Judy B. and taught me.

It works like this: For only two payments of $19.99, you'll receive . . . No wait, that's something else. Find a nice, thick rubber band that fits on your wrist but doesn't cut off the circulation (we want to get rid of certain thoughts, not certain appendages). Helpful hint learned from experience: You will want to have several thousand of said rubber bands readily available but out of sight of snap-happy family members.

Then every time you become aware of a negative thought—any negative thought at all—pull on that rubber band and let it snap against your wrist. See? *God just does whatever he wants.* Snap. *I really don't matter.* Snap. *It always ends up like this.* Snap. *Alone again, naturally.* Snap. At first it may sound like you're trying to start your own rubber band band. But don't give up.

> A person without self-control is as defenseless as a city
> with broken-down walls.
> —Proverbs 25:28, *NLT*

Keep in mind, the more we are aware of our own negativity or how much we agree with the enemy, the more we can help to stop it. At first, it might feel like we're trying to keep the sidewalk from getting wet during a thunderstorm by catching the falling rain in a Dixie cup. The job seems so impossible that no human could ever accomplish it. That's fine with God—he likes it when we want to be like his Son (1 Thessalonians 1:6-10; 3 John 11), and he specializes in projects that are God-size (for example, the exodus in the Old Testament and the virgin birth in the New). And take heart from the words of Abraham Lincoln: "The best thing about the future is that it comes only one day at a time."

Try This at Home or at Work!

Use the rubber-band-on-the-wrist method for one week. If you're a detail freak, tally how many times you snap the rubber band—though the blood blisters may tell the whole story. If you really want to keep track but are too lazy to do it yourself, tell your kids what you're doing. Although they cannot add simple equations like 4 + 3 in their math homework, their ruthless little heads will really get into this kind of math.

Did it surprise you how many times you snapped that nasty elastic loop in one week?

Do it for another week and compare. As you become extra sensitive to your thought processes, you may find you actually snap it *more*—I'm sorry!—because your thoughts are often negative in very subtle ways, and you simply didn't notice them before. At least that's how it worked for me.

Continue to do this for as long as you find that your thoughts are negative. Look specifically for the what-ifs or any of its relatives: the if-onlys, the yeah-buts, and when you say things like "I'll be happy if/when" and "Why does this happen to me?" ◉

REPLACE LIES WITH TRUTH

Think or, better yet, say aloud whatever truth you want to use to replace whatever lie you've been telling yourself. Use Scripture or rewrite verses in your own words, but say the truth several times. Let's look at a few possibilities:

"You make me glad by your deeds, O LORD; I sing for joy at the works of your hands" (Psalm 92:4). Simple enough, right? We are to do as King David did: look for what God has done—in our lives, in nature, in little gifts like pomegranates and sunsets—and recognize him for what he has done. Praise him and be grateful. But how often do we really look for the good in any situation, especially in those that seem burdensome (like too-long stoplights, yammery friends, countless loads of laundry, changes of plans, uncomfortable plane trips, etc.)?

Consciously looking for the good at this very moment instead of allowing ourselves to be irked, stressed, or traumatized might go a long way to renew our minds—making us grateful instead of grouchy, thankful instead of critical. (Psalm 126:2, 3 is another Scripture to use.) Try for a week to look for the good. Heck, really try to do it for 24 hours! I still can't quite make it . . . unless I sleep 23.9 of the 24!

> It was such a lovely day, I thought it a pity to get up.
> —SOMERSET MAUGHAM

"Be joyful always" (1 Thessalonians 5:16) and "Consider it pure joy, my brothers, whenever you face trials of many kinds" (James 1:2) are so hard for me to do. Someday I'd like to feel pure joy under all trials. Recently I was able to be grateful for a difficulty that happened about a decade ago. Woohoo! Hindsight happiness! We be movin' up! Find Scriptures to help encourage you to better things.

According to many sources, our retention rate breaks down this way (and I realize these figures are gross generalizations, but I like them): We remember 10 percent of what we read, 20 percent of what we hear, 30 percent of what we see, 50 percent of what we see and hear, 70 percent of what we discuss with others, and 80 percent of what we experience or practice. In other words, if you want to learn better, employ more senses. Duh.

Thinking a truth statement is good. Saying it aloud is better (but you might want to pretend to be talking on your cell phone at this point. No need to make the public question your sanity). Writing it down while you say it is even better. Explaining it to someone while you write it down looks (and *is*) still better. Best of all, reading your truth statement aloud in a crowd while standing, say, in a vat of chocolate syrup should make it really stick. (Get it? *Stick*? Syrup is *sticky*? OK, moving on.)

Ways to Replace Lies with God's Truth

When Luke Skywalker said, "I can't believe it," Yoda responded, "That is why you fail" (*Star Wars Episode V: The Empire Strikes Back*). Here are some ideas for success:

Idea #1—Purchase a little recipe card notebook (it has rings like a three-ring binder) and the cute little recipe cards that go with it. Write down Scriptures that would be good truth replacements for certain lies. Use various colors to code the cards, if you like. This is especially helpful when you're dealing with several lies. Keep the notebook in the car or in your bag. When a lie comes up, choose a Scripture to use to replace it and then say and pray that Scripture loudly and often. Beth Moore (in her video series *Believing God*) suggests pinning a card to your shirt, which is an excellent idea. I'm sure I would've thought of it myself . . . eventually.

Idea #2—Type a truth Scripture into your computer. Make copies and put those in various places. Or make the Scripture your desktop/screen saver. You want to keep that verse ever before your eyes.

Idea #3, my personal favorite—Write a particular Scripture on a batch of sticky notes and place them where you'll see them: on the fridge, on your bathroom mirror, on the TV, on the rearview mirror of your vehicle, on your child's (or spouse's) forehead . . . wherever you most often look. ⬤

Remember that while God's plan is to conform us to the likeness of his Son (Romans 8:29), the reality that we will ever be as perfect as our Savior is exceedingly, to the point of absolutely, unlikely (Romans 3:22-26). OK. So if we can't become totally healed and perfect *now*, why bother?

Well, imagine that you are a member of a really wealthy family. You have everything you want: the best toys, the latest techno media stuff, plasma screens playing cartoons and movies and video games. Junk food is brought on demand. The place is outfitted with comfy couches, a pool table, a foosball table, and Pizza Hut. There's just one catch: the housekeeper's a clutter nazi, so everything—all your toys, all the food, *everything*—has to stay in the play zone.

At first it's great: all of your favorites surround and envelop you. But soon you notice that you're lonely. Sure, your father comes to visit every day; but there are distractions, so it's hard to talk. You hug him, and he plays a video game, but you can tell it's not what he wants to do with you. Daily your dad asks you to go with him—you two could hang out in the other side of the house or take a drive—but you think it will be boring compared to the colorful, frenetic activity of your playroom. *Why can't everyone just stay in here with me?* you wonder.

Yet deep inside you know that you don't sleep well in the zone, and the food isn't the best. (You might even wish for a few carrots sometimes, but it's a passing thought that you quickly dismiss.) So although you're starting to outgrow the furniture and the noise kind of bothers you occasionally, this is where you stay.

> A man who views the world the same at fifty as he did at twenty has wasted thirty years of his life.
>
> —MUHAMMAD ALI

Think of all you're missing—discovering new places, trying exotic foods, seeing wonders, meeting people, climbing mountains, sharing dreams and laughter and tears with your daddy. Think of how awesome it could be, how close you could become just by listening to what the other is *not* saying, how you could go on endlessly astounding adventures throughout this amazing world. A choice eventually has to be made.

Just like the dad in that parable, your heavenly Father can call you by name, can hold your hand as you step out of the comfortable safe place you've made (of course, it will only be *after* you get away from it that you will see it as the prison it was), and can offer you all sorts of exploits and experiences with him. But you still have to try to put one foot in front of the other to walk through the door. (Whether you get out of that door the first one hundred tries is immaterial. After the one thousandth failed attempt at inventing the incandescent filament, Thomas Edison said, "We now know a thousand ways not to build a light bulb.")

As we let go of the things that hold us back and as we are— here is the point of the last few pages—drawn closer to God, our relationship with him becomes deeper and sweeter. That's why we try.

CELEBRATE VICTORIES

What happens next? Be grateful. Be grateful for how far you've come, how far God has brought you. Take note of it. Call it a victory. No matter how eensy-weensy the step feels, it's still a step toward God, toward truth, toward real freedom and healing. Be thankful. Rest. Repeat.

> I believe humans get a lot done, not because we're smart, but because we have thumbs so we can make coffee.
>
> —FLASH ROSENBERG

Be warned: The more truth that is put in place of the lies, the more you will be changed. The enemy will not have the hold he once did. Of course, that will make him gleeful and cooperative and willing to leave you alone, won't it? Um . . . that answer would be no. So know that attacks will come. Be ready for them. Pray. Keep Scriptures and phrases handy. Be aware of your weaknesses. Then when the enemy hits, you'll be able to stand (Ephesians 6:10-18). That really cheeses him off.

There comes at least one point during your overcoming of any negative emotion when you feel tired and "done." Know that everyone who works on cleaning themselves out will experience this on a semiregular basis. At my worst I felt done only three times each day: morning, afternoon, and nighttime.

 **STUFF**

A Case Study in Grateful Progression

Being thankful is powerful, but difficult when things are tough. I've been there. Jean Giraudoux said, "Only the mediocre are always at their best." But when you're in the midst of just trying to lift your head off the pillow, being appreciative seems like a ridiculously impossible thing to do. And it is, really. But as a discipline, being grateful is stunning . . . and necessary.

I started with the obvious: "Thank you for my daughter." "Thank you for the sunshine (or rain)." "Thank you for food." "Thank you, especially, for Diet Coke."

Then I got cheeky: "Thank you for keeping me alive (even though I wasn't always sure I wanted to be)." "Thank you for my husband (even though there were days . . .)."

Soon I was thanking him for crazy things: "Thank you for that little hummingbird who nearly hit me just now!" "Thank you for Meghan's learning 'struggle'—it keeps us both humble." "Thank you for helping me be thankful, even when I don't feel like it."

Finally came the big 'uns: "Thank you for this fight with fear; I'm not sure why I had to go through it, but I'm a different person because of it." "Thank you for that panic attack just now. It may not be from you, but the Bible says to 'give thanks in all things,' so that's what I'm going to do, even though I feel stupid. Thank you, Lord." "Thank you for the losses I have felt. I wish they weren't there, and I still don't understand. But I'm gritting my teeth and thanking you. Help me." △

Even though there may still be struggles, each time that we refuse to believe the lie and instead choose to believe the truth is a miracle step. It changes us down deep, even if it is one cell at a time. (That would be a good southern gospel song: "One Cell at a Time, Sweet Jesus.") And that means we are becoming more like our big brother Jesus, which is exactly what the Father wants for us.

We will begin to think differently, see things differently, see *ourselves* differently, understand life and the world through God's eyes; we'll become more fearless, more joyful, more patient and kind, more loving. We will become wonders, magnets that draw people to us and to Christ because of our responses and our lifestyle.

It's that easy! OK, off you go. The rest of the book is really not needed. You'll do just fine. Thanks for reading. Buh-bye now!

> One only needs two tools in life: WD-40 to make things go, and duct tape to make them stop.
>
> —GEORGE WEILACHER

Wait! I was just kidding. This is the start of an amazing journey, but there are some other tools you might find helpful.

FEED YOUR SOUL

We (OK, *I*) typically pick up the Bible, read a little, and call it Bible study (or the ubiquitous quiet time). But if those scant moments spent in the Word don't bring us closer to God somehow, then we need to try something new. I don't want to discourage you from doing your daily fifteen-minute Bible reading; I want to encourage you to add another dimension. The next time you do a read-through-the-Bible program or even a read-through-a-particular-book-of-the-Bible, pick out all of the names of God . . . or the descriptions of God. Or look for the promises God has made to his people throughout Scripture. Get a notebook (or use the computer) and write this stuff down. Then review these lists often. Get to know your Father. It's worth the time and effort.

One summer years ago, I read through the entire Bible, cover to cover. OK, not *exactly* cover to cover; it was more like from after the table of contents to before the maps. It was good to see how things were so interconnected, even in the midst of tough books like Leviticus and Deuteronomy. I then found a Bible arranged in chronological order. Although sometimes you can't really find a specific Scripture in there to save your life (or to win a trivia contest), it's great for giving a sense of which biblical-type guy was talking to which group of Hebrews when.

Isaiah 55:11 says, "My word . . . will not return to me empty, but will accomplish what I desire and achieve the purpose for which I sent it." Which means just what it says, doggone it. The Scripture gets beyond the "feeler" and the "thinker" and into a deeper part of you—a part greater than your emotions, a part that controls all things, including your ability to recall phone numbers of neighbors you didn't even like twenty years ago.

Why not bathe yourself in something that promises to work even when you don't understand it? Test God and his living Word! He's up for the challenge.

There are a number of wonderful tomes available that help us learn more about God. I like A. W. Tozer's *Attributes of God* (two volumes) and his *The Knowledge of the Holy*. The *Attributes of God* books are slightly more cerebral, but worth the effort. *The*

Knowledge of the Holy is a small, incredible book. And of course there's Max Lucado, C. S. Lewis, and John Piper, just to name a few of my favorites—each veritable founts of insight from which to drink deep.

> I've given up reading books. I find it takes my mind off myself.
>
> —OSCAR LEVANT

Kay Arthur has done several Bible studies, one of which is called *Lord, I Want to Know You* and is very good, especially with a group. Better yet, join a Beth Moore Bible study. She does a great job of revealing magical nuggets in Scripture. Each of her studies is offered on DVD or video and is challenging, enlightening, and fun. (Don't tell anyone, but when I grow up I want to be Beth Moore. I'm working on the accent right now, y'all!)

LOOK AROUND YOU

One of my favorite things to do lately is to look for God's gifts every day. For example, I love birds. I saw my first Eastern bluebird several years ago when we moved to Kentucky. Recently, my neighbor, Mr. Weldon, gave me a little bluebird house with detailed instructions on where, when, and how high to hang it. (Don't laugh; apparently bluebirds are picky!) Now there's a nest, and a couple of birds are busy darting in and out. Each moment of seeing those daintily painted bluebirds became a "kiss" from my Creator.

I've even caught glimpses of the elusive indigo bunting and scarlet tanager in our neighborhood. What a big hug from Heaven! Hummingbirds, goldfinches, and woodpeckers perch and fuss outside my window around their feeders. Another little smoochie. And just yesterday a cardinal pair sat on my deck and gave each other kisslike pecks on the beaks. Aww! Thank you, Lord!

> There are some days when I think I'm going to die from an overdose of satisfaction.
>
> —SALVADOR DALI

On days when I cross off something from my endless to-do-urgent-like-isn't-everything list, I think of that as another love pat. When homeschooling goes well and Meghan and I both learn something new—that's some *big* sugar from God. Sunny days with the windows open. Snowy days with the fire burning. Meghan's neck-breaking hugs. When I get a little further on a quilt, when I sleep through the night, when I go someplace while being a little less stressed . . .

You see, there's no contract that says I will always be healthy—many friends I know aren't. It's not a God-given guarantee that I'll be married—a number of my dearest friends aren't, or aren't anymore. I may not always be able to work from home and teach Meghan—lots of women I know feel they can't afford to do that.

I must take time to focus on those good things God has given me and on those moments of undeserved favor the Creator daily grants. Slowing down to spend a minute being thankful for *this minute* helps immensely to renew my heart and mind.

LEARN TO LAUGH

Another indispensable tool to help in this battle is to learn to deal with yourself differently. Consciously find ways to lighten up, let go, lose focus on yourself. And oh yes, relax. Wow! It all sounds so trite, but that's only because it is. A moment of shallowness can do much to give us a fresh viewpoint, especially concerning our scared silly little selves. And it mostly uses alliteration! What a bargain you're getting—not only is this author shallow, she doesn't rhyme!

TAKE YOUR MEDS

Consider Psalm 126:2:

"Our mouths were filled with laughter, our tongues with songs of joy. Then it was said among the nations, 'The LORD has done great things for them.'" ◖▶

Reliable experts say that people who struggle with fear (and its cousins: depression, anger, guilt, and self-loathing) often take themselves and everything else *intensely* seriously. So prove the experts wrong. Find ways to bring bits of humor and joy into your life, and see if you continue to stay fearful and depressed.

Also be on the look out for "they," an invisible but powerful group best exemplified in the phrase "You know what *they* say." Apparently "they" write for the extremely popular news group Somewhere ("I've read/heard it Somewhere") and know a lot of people named Someone ("Someone told me . . .").

"They" are a dangerous group proffering dramatically exaggerated information on what is important/appropriate/ correct. (I'd like to infiltrate their ranks. Wouldn't it be great to tell people, "Psst. I'm *they*." At the very least it would look good on a résumé.)

So here's a challenge for you: Don't dust the furniture this week; in fact, don't dust it until you can write messages in the grime. Then leave a note to your family members. See if they notice. Watch them closely; perhaps one of them is part of the infamous "they." If so, let me know.

Jana, a dear friend of mine, was recently diagnosed with MS. As she researched ways to beat this awful illness, she found something astonishing. Laughter helps heal.

Dr. Ann Weeks, a nurse/family therapist (DNS, RN) and engaging speaker, told Jana's group about a study she did among thirty-eight of her hypertension patients. Dr. Weeks prescribed at least fifteen minutes of deep, hearty laughter, three times a week. This could come from watching videos, reading books or comic books, or going to a comedy club. At the end of her study, eight patients went off their high blood pressure medicine completely, and the other thirty were able to cut their meds to varying degrees.

> The human race has one really effective weapon, and that is laughter.
>
> —MARK TWAIN

In fact, there is a whole segment of the health community that backs her on this. They are, as we speak, doing research on laughter and healing. (Wouldn't you love to be one of their subjects?) Humormatters.com and the Association for Applied and Therapeutic Humor (aath.org) are official Web sites for humor therapy. And although they don't send out free clown noses and whoopee cushions, they strongly suggest that laughter can speed the healing of various maladies . . . AND is specifically useful in reducing anxiety and phobias. So yuck it up! Doctor's orders!

Norman Cousins said, "Laughter is inner jogging." When we allow ourselves the luxury of laughter, a number of good things happen:

1. Good chemicals, the names of which are too long and

boring to mention, are released into the brain—similar to those released when we exercise.

2. Pent-up frustrations are liberated, causing muscles to relax.

3. Stressful thoughts and emotions are often cleared from the mind (at least for a while), so we think better.

4. Erroneous and damaging thoughts that have fueled fearful behavior can be seen for what they are. This allows a person to begin sooner to deal with such harmful thoughts.

5. People prefer being around those who laugh, so the way is paved for more friendships.

6. We begin to like being around ourselves, which is immeasurably helpful since we tend to be stuck with us for, like, our entire lives.

Note: Laughing doesn't necessarily *cure* anything, but it does allow us to relax into a frame of mind that provides a place for healing. Fear is a vicious cycle. The more we fear, the more seriously we take things. The more serious we are, the more fearful we can become. Humor can, if nothing else, help break that cycle for a bit. Besides, what other option do we have? As Elbert Hubbard reminds us, "Do not take life too seriously. You will never get out of it alive."

If you haven't already started a Komedy Kollection, it's worth the splurge. Many of my funny DVDs are also the favorites of families with sick kids or sick moms, or to watch during rainy and sad days. It's amazing how popular (and delightful) *Looney Tunes* and *Wallace and Gromit* and *The Complete Works of William Shakespeare (Abridged)* are.

I also keep books around that make me laugh. Some are sweet (Jan Karon's Mitford series is a delight); some are witty (Bill Bryson's *A Walk in the Woods*); and some are silly (*Dave Barry's Book of Bad Songs* and anything by Gary Larson). Find material that tickles you, and keep it handy.

SWEATLESS EXERCISE

Put Some Humor into Your Life!

Collect funny movies (they need to be funny to *you*).

Sign up for witty sayings on the Internet.

Read silly books or children's books.

Learn an Ogden Nash or Shel Silverstein poem (they're really silly guys).

Hang around people who make you laugh.

Tickle a toddler.

Carry a prop (a clown nose or bubba teeth) to be used when needed.

And laugh at yourself. Start with this fortune, actually found in a fortune cookie: "You appeal to a small, select group of confused people."[1]

I'm not a giggly person, but I try to make myself wrestle with Meghan and Kevin. They delight in surrounding me, kissing and tickling as I grimace. Secretly I love it, and more importantly, I need it. I love what Og Mandino said: "Laugh at yourself and at life. Not in the spirit of derision or whining self-pity, but as a remedy, a miracle drug, that will ease your pain, cure your depression, and help you to put in perspective that seemingly terrible defeat and worry with laughter at your predicaments, thus freeing your mind to think clearly toward the solution that is certain to come. Never take yourself too seriously."

> If you can't make it better, you can laugh at it.
> —ERMA BOMBECK

Try to find the absurd in any situation. One day Kevin and I were in charge of showing a DVD for our adult Bible class. Since my husband and I are part of a team that actually makes movies, you'd think we'd be able to show one. But no. The projector went down four times, there were problems with the video image . . . nothing seemed to go right. I was mortified. Kevin just laughed. He said that after a few minutes he realized there was nothing he could do, so he kept count of how insane the event might get. Out of a thirty-minute video, not even two minutes were really watchable. But Kevin just shook his head and chuckled through it all. I'm going to be like that someday.

Friends can be mirth makers. You need people in your life who can lift you up, encourage you, and gently remind you to work on healing, but who do so in the midst of humor. Remember what Mickey Friedman said: "Never give a party if you will be the most interesting person there."[2] I'm not saying that we shouldn't help those who are struggling; but if you don't have people with whom you can enjoy a moment on this journey, you are missing out on a lot of joy and health—and possibly putting yourself at risk for angst and despair.

LET GO, GRIEVE, AND FORGIVE

As Jesus shows you areas that need work, there are three emotional responses we may forget or want to overlook: letting go, grieving, and forgiving.

Learn to let go. This sounds ridiculously simple. *Letting go* presupposes that we are holding on to something. What do you have your emotional fists clenched around? Safety? Your children? Security (like money or things)? Your looks? When you worry, what are you holding on to? I don't know about you, but I tend to cuddle right up with those negative thoughts, false expectations, bad news reports—the what-ifs of my imagination.

I also have a death grip on the need to always be safe. What a white-knuckler, that one! I need to let these things go. They are toxic and deadly—might as well inject myself with E. coli or something. Holding on to negative thoughts and emotions force-feeds the lies that keep us stuck tight in the horrible cycle of unbelief and non-trust, thus assisting God's enemy in destroying something God loves. Er . . . that would be *us*.

Allow yourself to grieve. Let's see if I can explain this. Um . . . no, I really can't. So I'll try to describe it. OK, here's the deal about grief: There have been things in my life that haven't worked—decisions that were, to put it technically, poopy; situations that ended, to put it exactly, poopy; dreams that were crushed; hopes that seemed dashed; pain that felt overwhelming. These were, to use a repetitive but descriptive phrase, poopy. Such things, especially the ones that would be considered losses, need to be mourned. Even a dream that is born in you, if it doesn't "get borned" into the world, needs to be grieved.

> Laughter and tears are both responses to frustration and exhaustion. . . . I myself prefer to laugh, since there is less cleaning up to do afterward.
>
> —KURT VONNEGUT JR.

If you don't think you have any unresolved grief, get your notebook and list all the things that you've wanted to do but have never done. Or dreams you had or hopes that were never fulfilled. It shouldn't take long for you, if you are warm-blooded and breathing, to be sobbing your face off—or at least feeling some sadness. If you start this list but sense it may be too much for you to bear, then do it slowly or take the time to see someone. A Christian counselor or a grief facilitator can help you weep through these losses and get rid of latent negative emotion.

This exercise can also work for memories—those times in your past when you lost something but haven't yet mourned—or the loss of anything precious to you. Believe it or not, all of this unfinished mourning feeds fear, depression, anxiety, and the lies that surround them. I know this is only a hit-and-run about such a huge subject; but listing and working through my losses has made a significant difference in my life, and I think it would be wrong not to at least mention it. You never know, paragraphs like these are where sequels are born.

We also need to learn to forgive. Ralph McGill said that Eleanor Roosevelt "got even [with people] in a way that was almost cruel. She forgave them." Forgiveness is another topic that needs its own book, but here's a mini version: Forgiveness is part of getting well. After you've mourned, you must forgive.

Biblically, forgiving others is an essential part of being forgiven (Matthew 6:15). And I hate being the bearer of bad news, but this step can't happen until we allow ourselves to feel. You have to feel the anger, sadness, fear, and loss, thus wading through the toxic emotions as you look at painful memories and strained relationships. Then you forgive those involved (including yourself). It has to happen with God's help.

I know this from experience—because I personally don't *want* to feel the pain and rage that has built up, especially from old wounds. But the truth is that, generally, if you want to forgive someone from the heart, you have to think about specific hurts, feel the emotion of that event, ask God to help you forgive the person for the hurt, and then have the Holy Spirit help you see that individual from God's perspective. It sounds simple, but it simply can't be done without God. At times it also takes the help of others. Join me in this journey—I think it will ultimately free us from shackles we had forgotten existed. Plus it'll give me someone with whom to whine.

> Resentment is like taking poison and waiting for the other person to die.
>
> —MALACHY MCCOURT

Beating fear on the emotional level will necessitate capturing our thoughts, replacing them with the truth, looking for the kindness of God, laughing often, mourning what the locusts have eaten (see Joel 2:25), and forgiving ourselves and others for things that might have contributed to our present state of being.

I'd write more, but I have a date with Bugs Bunny.

TAKE YOUR MEDS

Memorize Psalm 56:3, 4:

"When I am afraid, I will trust in you. In God, whose word I praise, in God I trust; I will not be afraid. What can mortal man do to me?"

1. Grab your notebook and record one thought about this chapter, one positive thing that happened today, one Scripture that you like, and one way that God has blessed you.

2. What struck you as interesting or unusual in this chapter? Why?

3. Choose one Scripture that you will try to memorize. Write it down.

4. Did you participate in the imaginary argument described in this chapter? How did you feel? Have you ever done this type of thing before? Does it help you interact with the other person in real life? Explain.

5. Did you write out a list of unfulfilled plans, dreams, and hopes? Can you describe how that went? Were you able to mourn the losses?

6. What makes you laugh? With a friend, discuss favorite funny activities, movies, and books.

7. Discuss the topic of forgiveness with some friends. Begin to list the names of people you might need to forgive from your heart. Read Scriptures on forgiveness. Commit to pray about this with someone, if at all possible.

BEATiNG iT
PHYSiCALLY

My therapist told me the way to achieve true inner peace is to finish what I start. So far today, I have finished 2 bags of M&M's and a chocolate cake. I feel better already.

—DAVE BARRY

During my battle with fear, I tried almost everything. Some things worked; others didn't. Some things worked for friends of mine who worry, but not for me. Some things that worked for me didn't for them.

This, our third phase of beating the lies and other negative influences, consists of tips and tricks that can be placed in that handy-dandy category of Physical Ways to Beat Fear—because they are things you can physically do (astute authors fearlessly call things what they are). I know this isn't a one-size-fits-all deal, so choose from the smorgasbord of options.

RELAX

Our bodies tend to react to stress by tensing up, preparing for that good ol' fight-or-flight hormone. We can help reverse this tendency by consciously learning how to relax.

Most people, when amped, scrunch up their shoulders like they are trying to cover their ears from below. I do it. All. The. Time. So when I become aware of being stressed, I check where my shoulders are located and then pry them off the top of my skull. So . . . relax your shoulders. Right now. Have a friend push them down away from your ears if you have to.

> Setting a good example for your children takes all the fun out of middle age.
>
> —WILLIAM FEATHER

Get a shoulder or back rub (known as a massage in swanky, high-dollar salons) to loosen all those tight muscles. Although your insurance company won't like me (not that they even care), consider this Dr. Marcy's permission slip for you to get a rubdown. If you really want to reach relaxation heaven, then get a chocolate massage and bubble bath at that spa in Hershey, Pennsylvania. I don't know what the spa is really called, but if you go to Hershey and ask around, I bet anyone can direct you. I've also been told you can just follow your nose.

 **SWEATLESS EXERCISE**

Sewing Project for You or Someone You Love

Homemade heating packs are exceedingly helpful in melting tight muscles and unwinding knotted nerves. Plus they make great gifts!

Take a piece of fleecy material about eight inches wide and twenty-one inches long. Fold the fleece in half (pretty sides together) and sew the long edges. "Turn the sock" so the right side is now visible, with stitching inside, and sew the long edges again.

Mix long-grain white rice with some aromatic essence. I use lavender. Pour the rice into the pack until it's about half full. Turn down and sew the remaining open end.

To use, heat in the microwave for about two minutes. Place on achy muscles. (Careful, it can be very hot.) ⚫

Breathing is another part of relaxing that we don't do well during a freak-out. I mean, we breathe, but we don't *breathe*. While checking your shoulders to see if they are hunched up around your earlobes, analyze your breathing as well. As you drop your shoulders, inhale deeply. Exhale. Again inhale; then exhale.

Can you tell a difference between breathing to survive and breathing to relax? People who are stressed often end up taking only shallow breaths. There are several reasons for this, not the least of which is IQ. I'm kidding! The amount of brain cells some strange psychologist thinks you have (or don't have) has nothing to do with the way you take in oxygen. The fight-or-flight hormones are to blame, of course; and learning to breathe deeply, even when tense, will help slow those little buggers down. I heard famous cooking person Paula Deen say that she used to keep a little paper bag with her so she could breathe into it during panic attacks in order to stop hyperventilating.[1]

> Sometimes I lie awake at night, and ask, "Where have I gone wrong?" Then a voice says to me, "This is going to take more than one night."
>
> —CHARLES SCHULZ'S CHARLIE BROWN

Try using Marcy's Instant Finger Relaxation Position Which Has Nothing To Do With Eastern Mysticism (MIFRPWHNTDWEM). Press your thumb to the index finger of that same hand. Push hard for five seconds. Relax. Now move the thumb to the next finger and do the same, letting your shoulders drop and your muscles relax throughout your body. But don't become so relaxed that you fall over! That will make me look like a bad expert— and we don't want that.

O . . . K. It's better if you do both limbs at the same time, but I don't want you to put down these valuable instructions. So try it right now with just one hand. Touch your left thumb to the index finger of your left hand. Push and hold; at the same time drop your left shoulder, relax your arm, roll your neck, and let your left leg relax and sag (in a good way). Take a deep breath. Let it out. Again. Now that you're a MIFRPWHNTDWEM expert with one hand, you can safely set aside this book and try it with both.

I find this exercise very helpful when I am sitting and waiting somewhere. And it's become so natural that I now do it without even thinking about it. Should passersby ask me what I'm doing, I just respond, "I'm MIFRPWHNTDWEMing," and they pretty much leave me alone.

 **SWEATLESS EXERCISE**

Begin an Adrenaline-Release Program

Start with breathing. Do you breathe correctly?

Lie flat on your back. (You can also do this standing up straight or sitting up straight.)

Place your hand on your stomach.

Breathe as you would normally. Does your hand rise or does your chest rise? (Hint: The correct answer is hand. If your chest goes up, you're probably not getting enough oxygen.)

Now begin slowly breathing in through your nose so that your stomach lifts your hand. Count slowly and calmly to five as you do this—before you pass out. Just kidding! Simply do it slowly.

Hold your breath for a count of five.

Slowly exhale through your mouth while gently pushing down on your stomach with your hand.

Repeat.

Start with three slow breaths and work up to twenty-five. As you get better at it, you'll be able to add other exercises that will help keep you healthy, fit, and alert.

See how relaxed you feel?

And it was easy! ⑧

Take time to stretch. Any time you can stretch out (whether standing, sitting, or lying down) will naturally help you adjust your muscles and remind you to breathe deeply.

Here's something to try when you are lying down: Lie on your back with your hands to your side. Take a deep breath and hold it, counting to ten slowly. Now, exhale with a big *whoosh*. Inhale, and this time tighten your feet and leg muscles. Hold it. Count. Let it out (*whoosh*) and relax your muscles. Inhale. Tighten your bottom muscles as tight as you can. Count to ten. Exhale (*whoosh*) and relax. On the next breath tighten your stomach muscles, tighter . . . tighter . . . you can do it! Count. Good! Let it out (*whoosh*) and relax. Now your arms and shoulders . . . same drill. *Whoosh*. Now your head and neck. *Whoooosh*!

Good job! You have just completed my total muscle relaxer. You should feel at peace and more calm.

REFOCUS

There are times when you can't do the total muscle relaxer or when the MIFRPWHNTDWEM exercise isn't quite cutting it. I'm thinking here of standing in line at the grocery store with a toddler or going through security in most major airports.

In situations like this, it's helpful to have a diversion. Experts claim that you can't think of more than one thing at a time; so if you force your mind to concentrate on something other than what is worrying you, you might be able to alleviate your stress long enough to harness your thoughts. We've talked about quoting Scripture or having something uplifting or humorous to watch or read. Again, there are times when certain things are not available to you. And sometimes books and movies don't work. For instance, I can no longer read in the car (especially when I'm driving!). It makes me, to use a highly medical term, um . . . urpy.

SWEATLESS EXERCISE

Instant and Convenient Distractions

1. Choose one of your five senses and focus on it. Say, hearing. What are all of the sounds you hear? Close your eyes and focus. Try to list the sounds. Go through each of your senses if you want.

2. Keep a pad of paper handy and make your lists (grocery, garden plans, honey-do, potential great song titles, miscellaneous things to do, places you'd rather be right now). The more detailed, the better.

3. At the dentist's office, count floor or ceiling tiles. Look for patterns.

4. Review your ABCs. Try to find things that begin with the corresponding letter of the alphabet. This worked fabulously when Megh was sick one time. We made it into a contest as we drove to the doctor's office. She not only won, it took her mind off the crummies.

5. Some psychologists talk about choosing a large number (like 2,011) and counting backwards.

The point is to take Ashleigh Brilliant's words to heart: "Try to relax and enjoy the crisis." 🚫

When other things don't work or aren't available, I depend on crossword puzzles. You could probably use sudoku puzzles, but I think they are worthless and stupid. I think this because I can't do them. Not even the easy ones. Though my twelve-year-old daughter and my seventy-year-old mother and nearly everyone else on the planet can do these maddening number puzzles, I am sudoku-challenged. But choose something—crossword puzzles, word searches, sudoku—and you'll be surprised how quickly time passes and how normal you can feel when your mind is captured like this. I now keep a cheap crossword puzzle book in my bag when I travel. (I also carry a sudoku book so as to look like a person who's with it.)

Handwork can also help keep your mind occupied. Crocheting has long been my handwork of choice; and as a result, all family members, including pets, now have about a jillion afghans of their very own. These things don't die—I'm beginning to suspect that they reproduce in the summer while put away in closets. Although my family begs me *not* to make more afghans for them, I will continue because it's vital for my survival. OK, I will continue to crochet afghans until my family *pays* me to stop. Think of it as a reverse hostage situation.

Be a people watcher when you're out and about. Try to determine what each individual is like, what he does for a living, where he is going, whether he is with someone, what his story might be . . . As you watch these folks, pray for them as God urges. Or make up a story about their adventures. This is a fascinating way to focus your mind, and it might surprise you what you can discern with precious little information.

MEDITATE AND ESCAPE

(It could be argued that this section should have gone in chapter 7. But I decided to put it here, so you'll just have to deal with it.)

Meditation isn't just for tree-hugging granola eaters. And you don't have to call it meditation. Call it taking a holiday, or more realistically, taking a holi-hour or taking a holi-moment. We call it "going to Aruba" at our house because that sounds exotic and cool, which is a constant goal of mine. Whatever you call it, the Bible talks about it (meditating, not going to Aruba or sounding exotic or cool).

Although the Bible doesn't use the word *meditate* many times, the idea runs throughout. In Joshua 1:8 and Psalm 1:2 (and other places in the Old Testament) the word *meditate* specifically means to "actively consider or reflect." The Hebrew word can mean "mutter" or "whisper" or "the common Hebrew practice of speaking aloud under one's breath even when alone."[2] Some experts say the word *meditate* in the Hebrew carries the image of a cow chewing on its cud. The point is to be active in having the Word always before you.

In the New Testament, the word *meditate* is even less visible. The closest idea comes from Paul when he wrote to Timothy (1 Timothy 4:15). There the *NIV* says "be diligent," but the *KJV* says to "meditate." The word conveys the picture of someone who is practicing for something, as the orators did in ancient Greece.[3]

Philippians 4:8 says, "Finally, brothers, whatever is true, whatever is noble, whatever is right, whatever is pure, whatever is lovely, whatever is admirable—if anything is excellent or praiseworthy—think about such things." The word *think* here can also be translated as *meditate,* although it is more of an accounting term related to banking. It gives the feeling of looking at actual facts, counting on things that can be counted instead of on imaginary theories. When we take time to think deeply on God's Word, it reminds us that he can be counted on.

A holi-moment will look different for each person, but music is often a very helpful component. As a family we prefer George Winston and Enya. You may like classical or nature music or Christian instrumental . . .

Some people have a special corner in their houses designated for times of meditation. They keep an oversize pillow to sit on and have candles or some other smell-good thing. I'm not that groovy. I sit on my bed or in a boring chair on my deck. Whatever the place, this time is for you to purposefully relax your body and your mind while concentrating on controlling negative thoughts and focusing on positive ones from Scripture. Some people have a little devotional book they read, and then they think about what they've read. Try taking a Scripture and doing the same.

TAKE YOUR MEDS

Meditate on the Word. The Lord insisted that Joshua do it. Look up Joshua 1:8. David did it (Psalm 119:27, 148, for example). Paul hints at it in Colossians 3:16 and Hebrews 4:12.

I would suggest that you have a routine for your time. Turn on a DVD for the kids, turn on your music, sit down, take a deep breath, read a little, close your eyes and think on some specific good thing or verse, and then pray. You could easily do this in the space of a cartoon show.

With small children, though, you may have trouble finding even a few minutes. Try a holi-mini-moment. As you sit with your kids watching evil TV, just close your eyes and check your breathing. Focus on relaxing your muscles as you rest there. Say a little prayer or recall a Scripture verse, and then reenter the world. Even those mini "Arubas" are invaluable and will help you replace the negative with the positive.

> A vacation is what you take when you can no longer take what you've been taking.
>
> —Earl Wilson

I sometimes imagine favorite places when I "go to Aruba"—the ocean or the Rocky Mountains or IKEA. You can mentally revisit a pleasant experience that holds special memories—like hiking to Laurel Falls in the Smokies, singing with Grandma in her porch swing beside the rosebush, or visiting the aquarium. Recall the view, the sounds, the smells . . .

Even when I use some Aruba time simply to read a fun book or something inspirational, I always take a minute to relax, breathe deeply, and pray. It's a way to take sanctuary, defined by Lemony Snicket (in *A Series of Unfortunate Events*) as "a small, safe place in a troubling world."

BE PROACTIVE

You can also harness your worry-induced energy by actually *doing something*. If you are struggling with certain upcoming events like an airplane trip, for instance, or going to a graduation or a Tupperware party, you can use some of your Aruba time to rehearse the anticipated experience in a positive light. Picture yourself getting ready and then attending said event with everything going well. The fancy phrase for this is *self-fulfilling prophecy*, which basically means that if you think about bad things happening to you, bad things *will* happen. If you imagine good things happening, that will often be the case. Remember to breathe deeply and relax your muscles as you practice the episode.

STRESS FREE QUIZ

Pre-Event Assessment

When you are getting ready to go somewhere, what goes through your mind? Check all that apply.

_____ I think about all the things that might possibly go wrong so I can be ready for them (meaning "so I can stress out about it all").

_____ I think about all the fun things that might happen—and become really excited.

_____ I think about the food that might be there, because I live to eat.

_____ I think about all the things I won't get done because I have to go to this silly thing, and that makes me crabby and bearlike.

_____ I think about (fill in the blank).

Begin a grateful journal, a book of blessings—or as Susan Jeffers calls it, The Book of Abundance. Start by listing all the positive things in your life. Don't stop until you record fifty or one hundred items (or two hundred if you want a challenge) at the first sitting, if possible. Then add to your list each day or each week. You want to keep before you the things that God is kindly doing for and through you.

Several experts suggest writing down all the things you are concerned about. Use index cards. Make sure you put a date on the top of each worrywart card. When you finish, put them away. Two weeks later, take them out and look them over. What things took care of themselves? What things still need some work? Make notes on the cards, date them, and put them aside.

As you go through this exercise over the weeks, you should find that many things that initially consumed your thoughts in a stressful way actually took care of themselves. Although the experts didn't suggest it, I would pray over each item, asking for God's wisdom and participation. Note on your cards what you prayed for and then see what happens in later weeks. Give the cards to the Lord symbolically as you put them away. And then aim to not fret about those items for the allotted time.

Other experts suggest making some sort of worrywart action list. Write down everything that is bothering you. (You might find using index cards helpful here too.) Keep writing until you can't think of anything else. Once you are done, go back through the list and divide the items up into these categories: 1) things over which I have no control, 2) things over which I have some influence, 3) things over which I am in charge, and 4) things about which I worry because that's my gift.

After you've put each item in a category, take categories 1 and 4, pray over them, and put them aside. They are things that you have to let go. Set aside category 2 for now.

Looking through category 3, begin to list action steps you can take for each one. For instance, I worry about Meghan's education. She has a unique way of learning but is home-schooled. Therefore, whenever I become displeased with my daughter's scholastic zone, I simply look in the mirror; it is there I find her teacher, principal, gym coach, and lunch lady. I am very much in charge of this area. This winter I worked on a number of action steps to help me be a better teacher and hopefully to help Meghan be a better student.

> I have a simple philosophy. Fill what's empty. Empty what's full. And scratch where it itches.
> —ALICE ROOSEVELT LONGWORTH

When you work on your action steps, remember you need to have a goal, one that is attainable. One of my goals for gauging Megh's schooling was to make sure she had the tools she needs to be a success in life. These will not necessarily get her straight A's in a traditional educational experience, however. We work on typing, which helps spelling as well as writing. We work on life skills like making menus, cooking meals, global time management in the form of making lists and losing them, emotional management in the form of art skills, and people skills like understanding personalities and conflict management. These will help her in the long term, although they probably won't tell her where Antigua is located or the molecular structure of potassium.

We aren't giving up on learning these other things, but I understand that her learning style is not mine and her future might not be based on how much she knows but on whom she serves. We also signed her up for the Stanford Achievement Test for her grade level to see how she is doing comparatively. And I started going to a local meeting of home-school moms, giving me something else over which to have angst. No wait, it actually helped me see other types of curriculum and what tricks parents use to get their kids into the groove. Having several action steps regarding Megh's education, both short-term and long, has alleviated a lot of anxiousness concerning school—at least until I have to order material for next year.

Now pick up the cards in category 2. On each card write what type of influence you have. For example, several years ago my husband hurt his back, and the doctor suggested he strengthen his muscles that support that area. I can't *make* Kevin exercise, but I can influence: I can pray daily for him, invite him for a nightly walk in our neighborhood, and challenge him to a regular sit-up contest. I'm not in charge of Kevin's total existence, but I can do something instead of being a worrywart.

(By the way, another option for these category 2 cards that you've laid aside is just not to bother coming back to them at all. You've worked hard enough.)

CHECK YOUR LIFESTYLE

Certain complex molecular compounds like caffeine, sugar, and various flavors of ethyl alcohol often cause more stress than they alleviate. Consuming these comfort foods containing said ingredients by the dump truck-load has caused us, as a nation, to become overweight, health-challenged blobs.

According to our definition in chapter 5, anything that is used to give us relief when we should be running to God for rescue is considered medication. Of course, the term *comfort foods* sounds nicer to most Christians than *heinously addictive stash*. "Drugs" such as hot, buttery bread (just slap me now), salty/oily chips (*slap!*), Diet Coke (*slap!*), and chocolate (*SLAPSLAPSLAPSLAP!!*) are just a few of my personal favorites.

And (you're going to *love* this) according to medical professionals (i.e., doctors), processed sugar, salt, and caffeine are some of the worst things to aggravate the chemical reactions in a fear-charged body. Bottom line: ingest this stuff and you could intensify the stress-filled feeling. If you're already amped up, cut down your intake. See if that helps a bit. And try, instead, some herbal tea, or take a holi-moment.

> Coffee: helping people do stupid things faster and with more energy.
> —SEEN ON A COFFEE MUG IN ESTES PARK, COLORADO

Sleeping and exercise are two more areas that can help or hurt as you fight fear. Not enough sleep causes no end of stress and stress-related symptoms. If you don't believe me, go to your local health care professional and tell him you are stressed out.

After he has a hearty little laugh (because everyone is stressed out, including himself), he will ask how much sleep you are getting, how much exercise you are doing, and how much is in your bank account. This last question, although it might seem rather personal, helps your health care professional plan his next purchase, which, depending on the size of your savings, might be a payment for his new boat, thus alleviating *his* stress and making him happy for a little while.

> A good laugh and a long sleep are the two best cures.
>
> —IRISH PROVERB

Sleep deprivation is a huge factor in any negative emotion. It's not rocket science. If you don't get the sleep your body needs, nothing—especially your brain—will work at its peak. When that happens, the feeling of being overwhelmed is likely to increase, along with the feelings of fear, depression, and irritation.

How can you get enough sleep? Well, I'm not sure. Personally, I have a routine for bedtime, but it still takes me a while to go down. If you cannot sleep, stop fighting it. Get up, have a cup of warm chocolate milk or relaxing tea, read your Bible, pray for people, sew, knit, do a crossword puzzle, or write out the list that's been bugging your brain. Do something, but stop *trying* to sleep. That just makes it worse. You can always get back to a better schedule tomorrow. Tossing and turning only stresses you out mentally, physically, and emotionally. Easier said than done, I know, but aim for not trying, and see what happens.

> Laugh and the world laughs with you, snore and you sleep alone.
>
> —ANTHONY BURGESS

I can go for several weeks with a very sporadic sleep pattern (four to six hours). During that time, I prowl around doing different overdue projects that wait for me—like, you know, the dishes or the laundry. If I really get desperate, I dust furniture. Usually my body corrects itself pretty quickly because it *hates* housework. But if your sleep is disturbed for a month or so, see your doctor. (You probably need a physical anyway.) He or she can make sure there is no problem linked to the insomnia and can offer some good meds, if need be.

Some people who struggle with worrying thoughts and stress at bedtime have found that running a fan as they try to fall asleep is very helpful. Perhaps the white noise covers up the bangs and creaks of the night. I haven't tried it, but it sounds like a great idea.

Some experts suggest making your schedule for the next day before you go to bed. I used to do this, but my husband and friends made fun of me. And anyway, I had a kid. Parenting, if you don't already know, causes you to lose vital brain cells linked to organizational skills. The more you parent, the fewer organizational brain cells you have. That's why grandparents are so fun—they have roughly the same number of those brain cells as their third-grade grandkids. I can't wait.

 **STUFF**

Some Helpful Sleep Aids

Drink herbal teas that contain certain relaxing ingredients like chamomile. Celestial Seasonings has some good ones.

Do *gentle* stretching exercises. (Strenuous exercises will wake you up.)

Have some sort of routine every night—it helps your mind know it's time for bed.

Lie in bed and read. No TV and especially no news!

Take a warm bath.

Drink some warm milk. (Yes, you can add a little chocolate.)

Take two calcium (with magnesium) tablets several hours before hitting the sack.

I've heard melatonin is good. (Check with your you-know-who.) ⚠

Exercise, although one of the best helps in fighting stress, fear, and depression, is my nemesis. We won't go into it because we already have and it bums me out. If you don't exercise regularly either, then we are both lazy slugs. I'll promise to get better if you will.

Of course exercise helps you sleep better. It gets your blood going, which aids digestion and the cleaning of the body; it works your vital organs in a way that makes them stronger; it cleans out your lungs; it keeps those extra pounds off; and most importantly, it looks impressive. No wait! That's *not* the most important reason, but it's the one that might spur people like me to work out.

> When I feel like exercising, I just lie down until the feeling goes away.
>
> —ROBERT M. HUTCHINS

Earlier we said that adrenaline is one of the main chemical by-products of being afraid (or angry). Too much + too long = bad. Exercise, I'm sorry to say, is just about the only way to get rid of all this excess. However, if you exercise like a maniac, you may be using up valuable "exercise molecules." Since there are only so many of these little guys available in the world, you may be taking someone else's share. If you're going to do that, please take mine—I don't mind donating to a worthy cause.

No really, too much exercising may be as bad as too little if you're using it as a way to avoid dealing with your struggles and issues. (Can we say medication?)

PRACTICE

As with any new skill, keep practicing in order to improve. The goal is to capture the negative thoughts and stop the what-if cycle a little earlier each time such thoughts come up.

My friend David Yoho is a professional motivational speaker. I asked him how to beat fear and depression; and of the many wonderfully motivational things he told me, one specifically stood out. He said that when people ask him how he's doing, he always responds, "DOING GREAT!" (He really does talk in capital letters. Honest.) He says that responding like that is as much for him as it is for the people asking. He needs to remind his brain how well things are going because otherwise it's easy to be overcome by the negativity surrounding him. Not a bad idea—and one I'm trying myself (except without the capital letters . . . for now).

> A positive attitude may not solve all your problems, but it will annoy enough people to make it worth the effort.
>
> —HERM ALBRIGHT

Roger Von Oech said, "Everyone has a 'risk muscle.' You keep it in shape by trying new things. If you don't, it atrophies. Make a point of using it at least once a day." So another of my suggestions is to do something every day that stretches you, even a little bit. Read a new book, do something slightly different, try an exotic food, introduce yourself to someone you've never met . . . Each of those moments helps develop your risk muscle.

> Do one thing every day that scares you.
>
> —ELEANOR ROOSEVELT

Fear and depression make us not want to try things, but giving in closes down our little world even more. Of course, fears increase with doing something new because what-ifs surround the unknown. So don't attempt bungee jumping on your first day of being fearless. Just drive across town. Or simply sit on the horse. Attend a one-day seminar or tour the campus instead of signing up for a whole semester of classes.

Taking small steps (real or in your imagination) will help you take bigger steps. But know you must keep taking steps. If you don't stretch that risk muscle, it will automatically shrink.

Focus on the moment. Be present, right now, where you are, 100 percent. That's an extremely valuable tip (at no extra charge). Don't let yourself eject from the moment to stress about the past or the future. Now is what you have. Stay here. Enjoy now. It quickly disappears and you'll lose it forever. Margaret Bonnano was right: "It is only possible to live happily ever after on a day-to-day basis."

MEDICATE IN A GOOD WAY

As you fight fear and its buddies, don't forget there are many good and proper drug-type tools available, which include pharmaceuticals of the natural and unnatural sort. Of course, these are unnatural in a good and proper, doctor-controlled way *only*, because this author is an upstanding American and does the right thing, regardless of what she might have done during her teenage years that her mother still doesn't know about.

Antidepressant and anti-anxiety drugs never worked for me, although I gave them every possible opportunity. However, several friends have been (and still are) greatly helped by their use. If your struggle seems overwhelming and has lasted more than a few months, consider seeing your family health care professional about some of the meds out there. When your body is depleted, especially after struggling for a long time, it might need help to get back in sync.

My advice is, read about the various types of anti-anxiety natural remedies. You might want to check with your family you-know-who about the use of herbs; however, my experience with traditional doctors on this front has been pretty unsatisfying. A naturopath (which is an herbal doctor) can be instrumental in finding the best way to employ natural healing methods—I've used them before and love them. Unfortunately, your insurance company probably won't agree with me, so you might have to pay for this yourself.

You can probably find most herbal remedies at your local health food store. Or you can find them on the Internet. I like vitacost.com (it's informative and nonstressful), but there are tons of other stores out there.

Here are my remedy choices:

- Celestial Seasonings herbal teas—the ones specifically blended to ease tension.
- B-complex vitamins—commonly called the stress vitamins.
- Dr. Bach's Rescue Remedy—Use a few drops on your tongue or put in water that you can sip. I can tell a difference almost immediately.
- Smells (called aromatherapy by groovin' types)—can help you relax. My favorite is lavender. Put a few drops in a warm bath, on your pillow, under your nose, in your homemade heating pack. Lavender is a key aromatic for peace and relaxation. Peppermint is an uplifting aromatic, but in a relaxing sort of way. Go figure.
- Red wine—aids relaxation and is also good for your digestion, heart, and muscles. However, as with many things (like chocolate cake, shopping, and March Madness), just because a little is good, a lot is not necessarily better. Large amounts of wine can contribute to heart trouble, liver disease, a lot of obese (and sluggish) fat cells, and can actually *increase* the feelings of anxiety and depression. If

that doesn't scare you silly, see what the Bible says about overindulgence in Proverbs 23:19-21. Make sure someone knows you're using wine . . . this can easily get out of hand.

- Peppermint—helps your tummy when it's not happy. If you struggle with a sour stomach, try this or some peppermint tea with a little honey. Or eat some old fashioned gingersnaps. The ginger in these throwbacks to grandma's days really eases tummy mumblings.
- Relora—is a newer anti-anxiety blend on the herbal market. I like it way better than St. John's wort.
- Theanine—is an amino acid that helps you relax. If you're taking Relora, you may not need this.
- Some newer products—seem to be appearing, which combine many of the herbs and vitamins in this list (Relora, B-complex, theanine, etc.). I haven't tried any and they may be expensive. But it's interesting that the trend seems to be that more and more companies are going after anxiety with these natural products.
- Vitex—is an herb to help women and their . . . um, womanly stuff.
- Warm chocolate milk—Use milk, not a mix. It's very relaxing.

Please know that I did get professional help at times because anxiety got the better of me. And once again, I don't consider myself as being extraordinary in the stress category, although I experienced panic that occasionally was pretty disabling. So if you feel like your struggle with fear (or depression or anger or whatever) is getting out of hand, get yourself to a professional. A Christian counselor is great. A prayer partner/counselor is terrific. Your family health care professional might also help. Don't let your condition grow into a huge phobia that crushes your world.

> If you are cold, tea will warm you; if you are too heated, it will cool you; if you are depressed, it will cheer you; if you are excited, it will calm you.
>
> —WILLIAM GLADSTONE

Beating the fears, worries, and what-ifs requires a variety of efforts, including physical efforts. If one thing doesn't work the way you'd hoped, pick something else and try it. Don't give up. You never know which one will make all the difference in the world.

Ralph Waldo Emerson said, "Finish each day and be done with it. You have done what you could. Some blunders and absurdities no doubt crept in, forget them as soon as you can. Tomorrow is a new day, you shall begin it well and serenely."

TAKE YOUR MEDS

Memorize Matthew 11:28-30 from *The Message*:

"Are you tired? Worn out? Burned out on religion? Come to me. Get away with me and you'll recover your life. I'll show you how to take a real rest. Walk with me and work with me—watch how I do it. Learn the unforced rhythms of grace. I won't lay anything heavy or ill-fitting on you. Keep company with me and you'll learn to live freely and lightly."

1. Grab your notebook and record one thought about this chapter, one positive thing that happened today, one Scripture that you like, and one way that God has blessed you.

2. What struck you as interesting or unusual in this chapter? Why?

3. Choose one Scripture that you will try to memorize. Write it down.

4. Select one of the worrywart activities described in this chapter, and do it.

5. How's your breathing? Create a report to share with someone.

6. Which do you like better: crossword puzzles, sudoku, word searches, or something else? Why?

7. Read through Ephesians 4–6. List any directives that might help alleviate your negative thoughts and actions. Discuss them with a friend.

Remember to check the Resources section on page 247.

STAYiNG OUT
OF THE WHAT-iFS

The only completely consistent people are the dead.
—Aldous Huxley

So now that you've got it all figured out, we're done. You're perfect and will not be plagued by any other negative emotion. Yeah, right. And Santa Claus is bringing you a Ferrari for Christmas.

Will you *ever* be free from fear and its homeys? Personally, I think there will always be *something* to struggle through—to a greater or lesser degree—depending on your place in life, season of life, and moment in life. So basically, you'll be working on this (or similar stuff) for the rest of your days. Consider this the bad news.

The good news is that God is OK with that. The trick is to become OK with God's being OK with where you are at the moment—but without giving up on continually leaning into God and becoming conformed to Christ's image. God gives you the kindness of the process, however long it takes and whatever it looks like. Maybe you should too.

> This taught me a lesson, but I'm not quite sure what it is.
> —JOHN MCENROE

Picture this: A rocket checks and corrects. It can't reach its target in a single straight line. So as it travels through the sky, it moves a little bit, checks the coordinates, corrects its path, and then moves some more. This is repeated a hundred thousand times in order for the missile to stay on target.

We are no different as we aim for wellness, or really as we aim for anything. Check and correct. No judgment. No trauma. Just checkin' and correctin'.

Come to think about it, we can even apply this to our mistakes. Every action is a direct result of what we know. Saying "I should have done such and such better" isn't being realistic or truthful. If we had known to do such and such differently, we would've done so.* The end. Our behavior generally is *modified* as we learn; each encounter is an opportunity for gaining knowledge in how something is best done (or not done). It might be more accurate to say, "I know what works (or doesn't work) for the next time." We're just checkin' and correctin'.

I think we could create a new greeting for all stress-recovery individuals. "Hi, Steve. How's it going?" someone asks. "I'M GREAT!" you respond. "Just checkin' and correctin'. And, um . . . my name's not Steve."

*My husband pointed out that halfhearted efforts that bomb essentially disprove my theory because we actually knew what to do but didn't do it. I think that if we *really* knew that our schlumpy effort was going to result in bombage, we wouldn't have done it in the first place, which means that even a halfhearted-leading-to-an-unsatisfactory-result effort is a learning experience: we learned it didn't work. We be checkin' and correctin'.

ENJOY THE RIDE

Remember to allow yourself more laughter and joy. I understand that they are two different things; but if you are like me, you can squash them both with equal fervor. It's OK to laugh. Joy is permissible. I had felt fear for so long that I didn't realize I was suppressing both laughter and joy.

It took me a while to understand what it felt like to be relaxed. Eventually I had to give myself permission to actually *feel* the emotions within me at any given moment, including happiness and joy. I almost needed a doctor's permit to laugh at something funny, and some days I still seem to need an Official Laughter License. But it's getting easier. I can even chuckle at *myself* sometimes. Whoa!

> Joy in one's heart and some laughter on one's lips is a sign that the person deep down has a pretty good grasp of life.
>
> —HUGH SIDEY

Another thing to remember is that fear (like everything) will come and go in cycles. You will struggle with something, have a breakthrough, and feel like you have it all whupped (cowboy lingo for "completely and irrefutably eradicated"). You'll cruise along for a while and then suddenly be surprised that—Hey! Look at that!—what you've whupped is now back, sometimes in spades (cowboy lingo for "preposterously astronomic amassment").

When that happens, stop, take a deep breath, try to relax, and then ask God what might be causing the resurgence. Are you overwhelmed? Have you gotten sloppy with your thoughts? Are you memorizing the tunes of old TV shows instead of Scriptures? Have you been getting too little sleep and too much caffeine?

Or it may be that you have stepped into a different place in your journey, and God is ready to peel another layer of gunk off you. Carl Sandburg said, "Life is like an onion: you peel it off one layer at a time, and sometimes you weep."

Or maybe you're about to be called into a new level of trust in God, and Satan is throwing more at you to keep you from stepping out. Or it could be something else. It doesn't matter, but know that these times will come. If you can keep that in mind, and even try to prepare, you might find that the attack is not such a jolt and the battle is not as severe.

> Life is like quotations. Sometimes, it makes you laugh. Sometimes, it makes you cry. Most of the time, you don't get it.
>
> —Anonymous

Remember that nothing is forever except eternity. You really have more choices in any situation than you might think. Take time to look for all the potential possibilities, no matter how unlikely. List them if you can, even the ones that seem outlandish. Fear and anger and depression tend to erase perceived alternatives. You *always* have at least two choices, regardless of your feelings—you can either deal with the worrisome thing or not.

Find Them and Thank Them

Take time to compile a list of the people who have made a significant impact in your life. Were you influenced by your grandma? your sixth-grade teacher? the parent of a friend? a former boss?

Then make a goal to, once a month, pick someone from that list and either call or write. Reminisce about what he or she did for you and how grateful you are for that investment in your life.

It'll mean the world to the person, and it's good for you too.

Brief recap of the last three chapters:

- You want to capture and stop the what-ifs (and other bits of negativity) earlier each time they run through your head. Replace them with truth, with the what-is.
- Allowing yourself to feel all the various emotions in a natural, non-accelerated way (feel them as they happen) helps to prevent a buildup of negative emotions.
- Nothing you can do can make God love you more, or less, than he does right now. Learning to see and accept God's love is a huge breakthrough toward freedom and healing.
- There will be hills and valleys (and potholes and even a Grand Canyon or two) as you get better and grow.
- God gets to say whether what you do (or don't do) is a success or failure. Let him say.
- Today doesn't equal forever.
- Do something each day that stretches your risk muscle.

Even though at times it feels as if you're the only one required to work on your junk, it isn't really true. God *does* say you are to work on you (Matthew 7:3-5) and leave the rest (whatever—and whomever—that is) to him (Romans 12:19; Luke 6:37; 1 Corinthians 4:3-5; Philippians 3:12-14; and Jude 24, 25). I wish I got to say how others *should* act or be handled, but I don't. I am to work on me—disassembling the skeletons in my own emotional closets, cleaning out the barrels of toxic mental waste from my own spiritual basement, and sweeping out the cobwebs of cruddy thoughts from the corners of my own mind.

God doesn't promise that the other people in your life who may seem to glow with Chernobyl-like toxicity will change, or even be required to publicly acknowledge their "stuff," or be so visibly overcome as a result of your Herculean efforts that they fall at your feet and repent. If you're not OK with that, spend some time asking God why. (I'll meet you there.) You probably have some other things (like maybe an unforgiving heart) that are feeding the negative thoughts, emotions, and behavior.

> Know yourself. Don't accept your dog's admiration as conclusive evidence that you are wonderful.
>
> —ANN LANDERS

TRUST GOD IN THIS LIFE

As with all changes, start with small things. You won't be able to completely alter your DNA in a week (it takes at least two). So just choose a behavior, look for the lie, and then start in. Do the same with any tip/tool you find in this book. Give it a try and see if it helps you. Get a DVD or borrow something from the library, make some pizza, and laugh. Take one moment when fear attacks, snap your rubber band, capture a few of those thoughts, and stop the fear. Even if you don't do anything else the rest of the day, that is enough. Unless you think someone's watching!

Straight up? I still struggle. I wish I didn't, but I do. And to be even more honest, I don't trust many people who say they are completely healed, especially of mental/emotional issues like fear, depression, and lust. These problems pop up so quickly in the deepest recesses of our minds—and are fed by so many things in our society today—that it seems almost impossible to totally eradicate them. Of course, you might be healed. God can do anything he wants. Or you might struggle only a little bit.

I think most of us will always have spots the enemy will want to poke at or, more importantly, that God might want to clean out. But whatever point you're at, don't forget to live (and laugh and love and all of those other things that are profound and people make into trite sayings to embroider onto pillows and sell on eBay) while you're working on, and waiting for, healing.

Here's the toughest bit—I saved this for last, being a sensitive and caring communicator. Truthfully, I'm hoping you've found ample tidbits and activities and have stopped reading, thus providing me with the opportunity to slip this next part in and not have to discuss or defend it—because I'm not sure how to do so.

What happens when the what-ifs happen?

Because they do.

A little girl walking home from a friend's house after a slumber party is kidnapped, raped, and brutally murdered. Someone walks into a restaurant and starts shooting. People you know and love get cancer. A pandemic or recession threatens. A couple close to you, who seemed to be so happy (or at least not entirely *un*happy) decide to separate. Planes and cars crash. People, including you and me, get sick, even when it's inconvenient like on vacation or . . . well, while living. Plans flop. Investments tank. Jobs evaporate. We fail.

What do you do when those things you've feared actually come true?

Well, first of all, most of what I have to say at this point is intellectual. I haven't had cancer, my daughter is healthy, and my marriage is still together. I've had failures, but I've not been ruined. I've tried and tanked; but it hasn't cost me my job, career, reputation, or family. I don't mind it staying that way. I'm not sure I'm brave or mature enough to be able to write about those things from experience. I don't know if I ever want to be.

Since I've not gone through such überintense stuff, you, the observant reader, may be asking, "So what does she, the supposed expert, know?" Well, let me help you with that. The answer is, and I say this as a true professional, "Not much."

I was gratified to be able to answer promptly. I said, "I don't know."

—MARK TWAIN

I have had icky-ish things happen. And when they do, I react in the same manner as many mature, upstanding adults—I call my mom. She listens quietly during my little whine-fest and then offers the age-old wisdom that her mother probably offered her in similar circumstances: "It'll all come out in the wash." One time I responded snappishly, "I wish God would use the gentle cycle." And my mother sagely remarked, "Maybe he is."

Regardless of my feelings, in the end God is God. And my job is to try to trust him, love him, and enjoy him forever. True health is when it becomes less about me and more about him. How does that help when someone you love has a mysterious illness—or worse? What about the pain of losing everything you've ever worked for because of a mistake in judgment or a vengeful, thieving employee or a lawsuit by a self-serving "friend"?

First, when the what-ifs happen, allow yourself the luxury of feeling what you're feeling. Crawl through the fear, anger, disappointment, or depression. This is just part of being alive. And Ann Landers taught us, "The real trick is to stay alive as long as you live."[1] Don't stuff those emotions or try to stop them—they will only fester. God is big enough to handle your feelings, however 3-D they may seem to be.

Easy for me to say, I know. But that's what God says too. Second Corinthians 1:3, 4 describes God as the "Father of compassion and the God of all comfort, who comforts us in all our troubles." Jesus said, "Do not let your hearts be troubled. Trust in God; trust also in me" (John 14:1). King David said, "Even though I walk through the valley of the shadow of death, I will fear no evil, for you are with me" (Psalm 23:4).

Second, when the what-ifs happen, it's not necessarily necessary to "get back on the horse." According to David Yoho, my professional motivational-speaker friend, we *must* focus (or allow God to help us focus) on the positives of any event, no matter how the event turned out. And we don't always have to recreate the negative experience in order to totally overcome it.

That has offered some comfort to me. I usually feel that things must work perfectly in order for it to count, and even more so if I've tried and failed. In this case, not having to get back on the horse means that I can move on to other moments and experiences without guiltifying over the past. Learn something and rock on. It's all checkin' and correctin'.

As crass and insensitive as it sounds, having a "good life" (meaning "happy without pain," "perfect without flaws," "successful without failure," or "otherwise without any suffering whatsoever") is just a modern, Western concept. Reliable historians and sociologists tell us that most other cultures throughout history understood that good and bad happen to everyone. They never would have thought to expect mostly—or only—good things to happen in their lives. I like what C. S. Lewis said in *The Problem of Pain*:

> The Christian doctrine of suffering explains, I believe, a
> very curious fact about the world we live in. The settled

happiness and security, which we all desire, God withholds from us by the very nature of the world: but joy, pleasure, and merriment He has scattered broadcast. We are never safe, but we have plenty of fun, and some ecstasy. It is not hard to see why. The security we crave would teach us to rest our hearts in this world and oppose an obstacle to our return to God: a few moments of happy love, a landscape, a symphony, a merry meeting with our friends, a bathe, or a football match, have no such tendency. Our Father refreshes us on the journey with some pleasant inns, but will not encourage us to mistake them for home.[2]

Maybe one reason we place so much emphasis on things being perfect on earth—and I'm only saying this because I do it—is because we've forgotten who we are and where we belong.

Many of us Christians appear to have lost our view of Heaven as our home and have fallen in love with this temporary housing. When difficulties come, we're surprised and often devastated. If we could get our minds wrapped around the wonders of Heaven and the perfection and stunning fullness it offers, we might actually want to go there. This would probably have a dramatic effect on our view of "here" and thus alter our idea of what would stress us (nothing), scare us (nothing), depress us (nothing), and otherwise traumatize us (nothing).

TRUST GOD FOR ETERNITY

Stephen Wright said, "I intend to live forever. So far, so good." Maybe I don't "get" Heaven, don't long for it, because I haven't suffered enough. Or perhaps it's because I view dying as losing things instead of going on to better things.

Or it could be because the hereafter seems like it'll be so full of . . . you know, *people.* Don't get me wrong. I like people OK, but I *love* animals and nature and books and good chocolate. And

I've worried that Heaven will not have any of those things. This all sounds childish, but it's true. I don't even know what I'll do there. In my head I know it is much more amazing and beautiful than I can imagine; but for some reason, it's hard to get excited about it deep in my earth-bound heart.

Behind all my thoughts, I'm surely believing a lie of some sort. I mean, the apostle John described Heaven as having streets of gold, foundations decorated with precious stones, and lightning and thunder coming from God's throne (Revelation 21:19-21; 4:5). How in the world could I think a place like that would bore me?

The Bible doesn't say Heaven should be what I think it should be, but I act like I need to put some sort of stamp of approval on the design before I get stoked. It just shows that at the base of my disappointment, disillusionment, or distrust is *me*. Deep down I somehow think I know how Heaven should look (because it's where *I'll* spend eternity, right?), and I'm caught up in details like whether there'll be books or animals . . . And although these are certainly worthy of thought, study, and discussion, I miss that the whole stinkin' goal of Heaven is for me to be with the one who is my Creator and my Father!

It's critical to your healing that you understand that Heaven's not about you—it's about me. No wait! I'm kidding!

I'm having difficulty making my point. The truth is that, in a way, it *is* all about me (God loves me, sent his Son to die for me, is designing my personal cabana for eternity) but SOOOOO totally *not* about me (I'm the creation, the recipient, the clay). When I can live in this truth, I can let God do his magic. And I'll be able to worship him no matter what my surroundings are.

I *am* going to Heaven. I *am* going to die someday. So are you. Atrocities, disease, natural disasters, and old age have occurred since Adam and Eve. That's when the trouble started.

> If real life was like the movies, I should have lived happily ever after.
>
> —Piper Laurie

What will your funeral be like? At some funerals, family and friends release balloons in the sky to celebrate the person's life.

For Christians, such an idea of rejoicing should be doubly—no, infinitely so. Paul said in Philippians 1:21, 23, "To me, to live is Christ and to die is gain. . . . I desire to depart and be with Christ, which is better by far." Many Christians have referred to dying as going home. Accepting the bad along with the good here on earth (see Matthew 5:45) as part of our journey home helps to make the bad not so horrible because it is not seen as an exception to life, and the good becomes a little sweeter because it is not seen as an expectation. This would also have the added benefit of allowing me to put stuff like "Without the bad we can't truly appreciate the good," "It is what it is," "No pain, no gain!" and "That which doesn't kill me makes me stronger" on T-shirts to sell on the Internet and still feel good about myself.

 **⚠ FRIGHTENING STUFF**

Death

What is your view of death? If you aren't sure, watch and see how you react even toward nonhuman death like deer corpses on the roadside, trees bulldozed at a building site, or broken home appliances like your ex-dishwasher. I'm not trying to be morbid, but I believe that most people who say that death doesn't bother them are lying. We can't get over a fear of death until we actually know whether we are afraid or not.

If you live in the US, you have been inundated with anti-death thoughts. People don't die; they pass on, are gone, pass away, aren't with us anymore, or have gone to that big golf course (or racetrack, garden, hot tub, McDonald's . . .) in the sky. We don't acknowledge death. So look death in the face, and check your own response.

Woody Allen once said, "I'm not afraid of death, I just don't want to be there when it happens." One way to deal with your own mortality is to make out your will. Do you have a will? Can I be in it? No wait! I just want to say that it's a good idea to write out the plans and wishes you have for your family and your stuff. Don't force those you love to make decisions about you while they are in the middle of their grief. ⚠

"Everybody wants to go to heaven, but nobody wants to die," said Joe Louis. What is the truth about Heaven? Well . . . do you think nature is pretty? I mean, are you amazed by animals, stunned by sunsets, and impressed by weird plants and huge mountains and vast oceans? According to the Bible, God made the universe, the earth, and everything in it in seven days. Jesus told his followers not long before he was crucified, "Do not let your hearts be troubled. Trust in God; trust also in me. In my Father's house are many rooms. . . . I am going there to prepare a place for you" (John 14:1, 2). If earth is this amazing after a seven-day creation, then just think how Heaven will be as Jesus designs, builds, and decorates rooms for you and me. After all, he's been working on it for nearly two thousand years!

And that's just the one truth I can think up right now! I need to bask in the truths about my eternal home, given by the Holy Spirit and found in the Word: that Heaven is real and will be something more wonderful and enjoyable and exciting than I can imagine; that Jesus has really been planning for my homecoming longer than it took to make the entire universe; that being there will answer all my longings and fill me up fuller than full.

Billy Graham wrote, "In my travels I have found that those who keep Heaven in view remain serene and cheerful in the darkest day. If the glories of Heaven were more real to us, if we lived less for material things and more for things eternal and spiritual, we would be less easily disturbed by this present life." When I think that way, then maybe, *just maybe,* my struggles here on earth might not mean quite so much because I know I'm not *really* where I belong yet. All believers can know that when we finally get there, our Daddy will be waiting to hug us and make everything all better.

> Someday you will read in the papers that Moody is dead. Don't you believe a word of it. At that moment I shall be more alive than I am now. I was born of the flesh in 1837, I was born of the Spirit in 1855. That which is born of the flesh may die. That which is born of the Spirit shall live forever.
>
> —DWIGHT L. MOODY

I have a friend whose son died six years ago. Debbie wants to be in Heaven so badly she almost shimmers. She called the other day, crying. "Six years is too long not to hug him," she sobbed. I listened sympathetically because anything I could have said wouldn't have been *sym*pathetic but simply pathetic. So I listened. And moaned. And listened some more.

Then after hanging up, I made a beeline for my own child and completely hugged her guts out. Poor Meghan, here's her mom blubbering and dripping, squeezing the life out of her. She finally gasped, "Hey, Mom. You're not OK, are you?" (Nothing gets past my daughter, no siree Bob.)

My dear friend *longs* for her real home—she doesn't want to stay here a minute more than God has planned because she *understands* what Heaven is all about: No more tears. No more separation. No more pain. No more fears. No more death.

I'd like to feel like she does—but without the hurt. I wish for a "heavenly pill": take it and get a glimpse of your eternal paradise. *Sigh.* It'd probably just make me grouchy cuz it would wear off and I'd still be here.

> Life is what happens to you while you're busy making other plans.
>
> —JOHN LENNON

Pain and suffering show up regularly in the Scriptures. Select someone in the Bible. Anyone. Bad things happened even to that person. Take Job. Lost all ten of his kids, his fortune, his health, and his livelihood. In fact, the only thing he didn't lose was his whiney wife. In the middle of the trauma, he said, "I know that my Redeemer lives, and that in the end he will stand upon the earth. And after my skin has been destroyed, yet in my flesh I will see God; I myself will see him with my own eyes—I, and not another. How my heart yearns within me!" (Job 19:25-27).

TRUST GOD FOR THE GOOD

Whatever the reason for the yucky things—whether they happen as a direct result of a fallen world, as the ramifications of bad choices, as a tool that God uses to bring us closer to him, as something designed to make us stronger, as a way to make us more aware of the good, or for some other freakish and unknown reason—they *do* happen.

With God's grace we can focus less on the whys (or why-nots) and begin looking for God's good in the circumstance. That's the only way, it seems to me, to stay sane(er) and healthy(er) as we travel through this life. As trite as that sounds, somehow it's true. Billy Graham had the correct approach: "I've read the last page of the Bible. It's all going to turn out all right."

Whatever you've gone through or are crawling through right now, I'm sorry. I wish I could fix it; I wish it were different; I wish I had a good explanation. All I know is that God is there, somewhere, whether it feels like it or not. Because he promised to be. God is good, even though this ride called the Christian life might scare you absolutely silly sometimes.

Big finish: Fighting fear or any negative thing is worth every bit of your, and the Holy Spirit's, effort. Dispelling the enemy's lies you've believed about yourself and God is vital in this process. It's important even if you don't have anything "wrong" with you (sure you don't!). Each time you reject a fearful or destructive thought or counter a lie with the truth, you allow yourself to be brought closer in relationship to God.

Someone once said that Hell is being alone with yourself forever. Then Heaven might be being completely out of yourself (that is, your sinful, unhealthy self) and into God forever, thus becoming all that God designed you to be, with every part of you totally pure and redeemed. Won't it be nice to finally not have to deal with this junk? I have moments when I can say, "I think so." And that's what Benjamin Franklin would've said. I'm sure of it.

TAKE YOUR MEDS

Read 2 Corinthians 1:3, 4 aloud:

"Praise be to the God and Father of our Lord Jesus Christ, the Father of compassion and the God of all comfort, who comforts us in all our troubles, so that we can comfort those in any trouble with the comfort we ourselves have received from God."

1. Grab your notebook and record one thought about this chapter, one positive thing that happened today, one Scripture that you like, and one way that God has blessed you.

2. What struck you as interesting or unusual in this chapter? Why?

3. Choose one Scripture that you will try to memorize. Write it down.

4. Do you have a will? If not, when can you make one?

5. When you started reading this book, did you have someone in mind who might benefit from the material? Who was it? What did you find that might be helpful to that person?

6. When the what-ifs actually happen, what else can be done to help get us through?

7. Read through Psalm 139 and list the ways David describes God's knowledge of him. Spend some time meditating on the fact that God knows you in those same ways.

8. Go back through your notebook and review your answers to question 1 for each chapter. Is there a theme to your answers? Can you see how far you've come in just this short a time? What was your favorite chapter, and how have you been able to use the information?

   Remember to check the Resources section on page 247.

EPILOGUE

MY NAME iS MARCY, AND i'M A . . .

As [a man] thinketh in his heart, so is he.
—King Solomon, Proverbs 23:7, *KJV* (also my mother)

T he above thought, although on the surface is a seemingly simple and innocent proverb, when applied to one's life can offer stunning revelations. By virtue of examining someone's behavior—let's say, hypothetically, *mine*—one can draw a conclusion about that person's thought processes. In my case the conclusion would be that, for many years, my thinketh stinketh. Even as recently as this morning, my thinketh stinketh, which is ever so irritating because I'm writing this book about overcoming fear and fearful thoughts, and here I am neck deep in wearisome worries and anxious attitudes.

Often—today being an irksome example—I am convinced, or at least deluded, that such thoughts and attitudes are normal or even upbeat. *Sure, I struggle with low self-esteem, but don't we all?* Or, *Yeah, I get depressed. But feeling fat and ugly seems to be a regular part of the collective feminine psyche, not to mention an incredibly effective tool used daily by advertisers (God bless them).* Or, *Surely you can't think I'm being pessimistic. I'm a* realist, *which is* hugely *different, but please don't ask me to explain how.*

> Be yourself is about the worst advice you can give some people.
>
> —VARIOUSLY ATTRIBUTED TO J. B. PRIESTLEY,
> TOM MASSON, MARK TWAIN . . .

As is typical, there's a particular region where my thinketh stinketh most severely—from where I can't escape into semantics and which no amount of makeup can conceal. As you know from the previous ten chapters, my fingerprint feeling, my demonstrative, live-in emotion has been fear. And fear entered into my life, as it did for most anxiety-ridden adults, while I was a wee young 'un.

I went to kindergarten in the mid-1960s during a gigantic upheaval that rocked this great country to its very core. This cataclysmic commotion ultimately reached every corner and nearly every house, business, and gathering spot. The thing that caused this disruption, this disturbance, was rock 'n' roll music.

Actually that wasn't it. I mean, there *was* a lot of yammering about this "devil music," but that isn't the upheaval to which I'm referring. In the mid-1960s, responsible people had begun to wage a war more difficult than the battles against rock 'n' roll and the Communist forces in Korea and Vietnam combined. I'm talking about the war against smoking.

At that time most everyone smoked; people puffed away wherever they wanted. Actors and actresses made smoking seem sophisticated and cool. Tobacco companies advertised in magazines, on billboards, on TV, and practically gave away trial packs. As far as I know, kids and pets were encouraged to hang out in their backyards, lighting up while waiting for Kick the Can to start. It was one of the certified hipster elements of the age and an approved way to stay thin. And most importantly for this chapter, my mother was one of the millions who enjoyed burning the aromatic leaf.

Then came Mrs. Hill, my kindergarten teacher at Westmoor Elementary School. As you'll soon see, I relate to Robert Fulghum's words: "All I really need to know about how to live and what to do and how to be I learned in kindergarten."

Mrs. Hill, being an extremely responsible citizen, decided to present her five-year-old charges with the dangers of smoking. She dutifully showed us glossy pictures of black lungs and people with smoking-related diseases like cancer and rotted teeth. She also displayed helpful instructional devices in the form of tar-coated sponges, jars of money spent on the habit, and an old ashtray to smell. I don't remember what all she said exactly; but it spurred me to superkindergartner action, driven by a fear I had never known before.

And so it was that one day I marched home and did what any young child would do in order to save her world—I started packing my bags. My astute mother inquired as to my puzzling actions. "*Sniff, sniff,*" I . . . uh, sniffed. "I won't stay here and watch you kill yourself with those awful cigarettes."

To my mom's credit, instead of splitting a gut, she quit smoking that day. But my fear of losing my mother took a long time to leave. The what-ifs had entered my little life.

A while later (what is time when you're a kid?) during the height of the Vietnam War, as I watched the horrible images and heard the adults talk, a terror crept over me concerning my baby brother. What if he were drafted? What if something happened to him over there? Though he was not quite six years old, I lay in bed crying and begging God nightly not to send him to that place of death. The what-ifs had struck again.

> It is never too late to have a happy childhood.
> —TOM ROBBINS

Many other things happened—some exciting, some devastating. But interestingly, it took getting married for this what-if worrywart to bloom into a full-blown panicked person.

Without moving into *National Enquirer* mode (motto: Who needs facts when you can retouch photos?), I really can't express the pain, fear, and feelings of worthlessness that exploded between Kevin and me during the early years of our marriage. Just understand, it was bad. We were toxic. And we were Christians. Chernobyl Christianity: a perfect setup for quiet, lonely, debilitating trauma.

The feelings of panic started small—a runaway heartbeat while in a nice restaurant, the desperate need for some extended restroom time while at the mall . . . Soon I felt stressed out through much of my day. I prayed to get better and fretted that things would get worse. My thinketh was more extensive than my prayeth; so (no surprise) worse the panic became.

> I don't suffer from insanity. I enjoy every moment of it.
> —SEEN ON A T-SHIRT

In the beginning I had no name for what I was feeling. But I was regularly sure I was dying—or going insane, which might have been slightly worse. Among countless other traumas, I was terrorized by the notion that I'd end up in the Home for Pathetic Women Who Shuffle Around in Colorless Hospital Gowns—head bowed, hair ratty, mumbling or drooling. Admittedly, my fears were logic-challenged.

My poor husband, who tends to be slightly more gifted in the logic-as-defined-by-having-a-Y-chromosome department, would try to understand my terror but always ended up just cocking his head and wincing, much in the same way he did when I once asked him to run to the store and buy me some you-know-whats. It wasn't connecting. Of course, his reaction made me feel even more worthless and stupid and added the fear of rejection to my fears. Oh, the wonderful circle of *strife*.

The crippling moments quickly escalated to multiple times a day—bringing on instant diarrhea, lightheadedness, and breathlessness. Sweating and shaking profusely, I would often feel faint and sick all at once. I felt pursued by a demon, so I couldn't sit still—I had to find someplace safe where I could breathe and rest. But where could I go?

And I was convinced everyone knew how pitiful I'd become: my husband must have thought I was being a baby; my family, I was sure, felt I was a controlling jerk; my friends probably assumed I was an eccentric bordering on a Howard Hughes wannabe . . . My dog, however, always thought I was the center of her universe and could do no wrong. (Thank goodness for dogs, is what I say.)

I was wrong in my assumptions of what others were thinking—no one *really* detected the award-winning freak show occurring in my head. It's a universal truth: folks rarely know how badly we suffer deep inside because we (all of us) often look upbeat and together on the outside. Unfortunately, I was far from it on the inside. Ultimately, the internal insanity won, shutting my world down.

TAKE YOUR MEDS

Memorize Psalm 34:18:

"The LORD is close to the brokenhearted and saves those who are crushed in spirit." ⬤▮

It doesn't take a rocket scientist to see what my mind was thinketh-ing during those years. Can you believe I thought I was funny and upbeat? Right. I was funny like the Grim Reaper is a stand-up comedian.

For nearly twenty years—during the height (or depth, if you'd rather) of my struggle with debilitating fear—much of my daily existence centered on trying not to freak out, throw up, or . . . well, let's just say I never needed a laxative. Eating was an act of sheer discipline—not because I might forcibly eject the calories to stay thin, but because I was in a constant state of terror that nauseated me. It's interesting to note that although I perpetually worried about it, I never did heave. Not once. For all the hours of mental and emotional trauma, not an animal cracker, M&M, or rice grain returned to see the light of day.

At one point, these fears (of becoming sick, passing out, burdening someone with my "problem," causing a disturbance in the Force) became so intense that I even had trouble leaving my house. It's said that King Louis XIV once remarked, when his carriage had arrived exactly on time, "I *almost* had to wait."[1] We laugh at the picture of someone whose day consists of anticipating the worst and then recalling that it almost happened. But that's how I was.

Going to the grocery store was its own unique brand of torture because I was afraid of collapsing (or freaking out) while I waited in line. Sometimes I filled my cart with provisions only to abandon it because the line was too long (*too long* in this case means "more than no one in it") and the panic had become overwhelming.

Shopping got a little better when the ten-items-or-less line was created, and the checking-out process went more quickly—unless there were any actual *people* with ten or less items in line! My favorite grocery store invention of the millennium was U-Scan. Most folks were too afraid to use it (finally—fear worked *in* my favor!), so I often had the whole area to myself. Sadly, this innovation eventually became a busy place.

Riding with people was another horror (it still ranks a close second to cleaning toilets). I was tortured with the thought that I might freak out in the car, leap out and run screaming and puking across a crowded mall parking lot or interstate median. Or we might reach our destination and I'd become sick and immediately have to go home, thus spoiling everyone's fun.

Eventually I came up with a splendid solution: take my own vehicle or don't go at all. And being immensely practical and a quick thinker, I could fashion very plausible "reasons" to always have my own ride or bow out, but they were a thin veneer coating the madness.

Looking back, being this psychotic should have been fun. Unfortunately, it wasn't fun *or* funny—it was torture. And my sweet husband still has his head cocked to the side.

> Strange as it may seem, my life is based on a true story.
> —Ashleigh Brilliant

Worst of all was the guilt. I knew how things *should* be. I knew what I *should* look like, how I *should* act, how a good Christian *should* live—I hated being weak and faithless and pathetic. And although I didn't know exactly what normal was, I knew I certainly didn't fit normal.

But I didn't do a good *abnormal* either—my clothes were

boring, my pet was the most common dog in the US (yellow Lab), my hair color was simply Sun-In with Lemon, my ears were pierced only once and the rest of me not at all. I didn't drink, smoke, or even cuss (OK, *occasionally* I used a colorful adjective, but it was *always* because of a very good reason). A vanilla loser, that's what I was—terrified of living and too chicken to die. It all seemed hopeless.

> Don't be so humble, you're not that great.
>
> —GOLDA MEIR

And my marriage? Because of my fear, Kev's frustration, and our toxic interaction, it was more wedding bomb than wedded bliss. You missed a nonstop party. That's all I'm saying.

Eventually, perhaps miraculously, *agoraphobia* surfaced in one of the dozens of self-help books I had collected. The definition seemed ridiculous: "a fear of open spaces." But the portrayal of the panicky feelings matched perfectly what I experienced many times in a day. I felt as if the author had been listening in on my deepest thoughts and emotions for years. Such mental eavesdropping had the potential for a great Hitchcock movie plot. The notion is extremely creepy, but at least a name was finally put with the insanity. Maybe I *was* going out of my mind, but so was someone else! Thank you, Jesus!

Once I had a way to help others understand what I was living with, the silence was finally broken. And the more I shared my struggle, the more I found out that I actually knew other people who were sort of like *me*! Maybe I wasn't a misplaced space alien after all (like Superman, only without the superpowers and the great cape, and of course, I *never* looked *that* good in spandex . . . *sigh*).

Medical help came next. Doctors offered antidepressants and then anti-anxiety drugs. Yee-haw! There were enough of us to warrant someone's creating medication! I was finally part of a majority. Or at least, I was the target of several TV commercials. Sadly, the side effects of each prescription were worse than the disorder. Wouldn't you know it? Drugs are available, but they don't work for *me*.

Although all these were steps forward, they seemed so few and far between compared to the gigantic backward leaps I experienced daily (which were connected to the panic attacks and the negative thinking). Eventually I decided to just give up. I would live and die ill. My husband and I seemed as far apart as two people could be and still share a bed. For my infant daughter's sake, I carried on breathing but had, in essence, quit living. I even started drinking; at least I didn't hurt so badly.

Yet oddly, in giving up and finally deciding to accept myself warts and all, there came a new sense of peace and another teeny dash of hope. "I will never leave you or forsake you," whispered Jesus. Maybe God hadn't abandoned me, and maybe Jesus could love me after all. I determined to bet my life on those two maybes.

Oh no! Not ANOTHER learning experience!

—SEEN ON A BUMPER STICKER

That was years ago. The steps forward slowly became larger and more frequent. The backward steps eventually became smaller. Fortunately, I continued to seek help via counselors (lay and professional) and Bible classes—even when I didn't feel like it. Friends and family prayed for me and loved on me, even from afar. Kevin and Meghan cared for and encouraged me, even during my most unlovable moments. And although I couldn't always see it, God never left me—not even for a second.

Through many God-ordained events, faith- and grace-filled people, and the proddings of the Holy Spirit, God started showing me where my fears really took me and what I *really* believed. With the help of good books, good friends, a good God, Spirit-filled prayer, and the Faces of Christ retreat at Southeast Christian Church in Louisville, truth began to shine deep into my soul.

Although I'm still on the journey, I'm more excited than anxious about the future and can actually say (on most days) that I can't wait to let you know how it all turns out.

 FRIGHTENING STUFF

Symptoms of an Anxiety Disorder

Check yourself.

Any or all of these symptoms can be caused by real, and serious, illnesses.[2] Consult your health care professional. If no physical cause is found, then consider treating the symptoms as anxiety while also looking for the cause of the anxious feelings.

Look for consistent and/or troublesome:

____ Dry mouth

____ Heart thumps, fast heartbeats, skipped heartbeats

____ Sharp pain or tenderness around the heart

____ Tiredness

____ Indigestion or rumbling of the stomach

____ Sweating

____ Needlelike tingling in the hands or feet

____ A choking or lump in the throat
____ Tight feelings in the chest
____ Inability to take deep breaths
____ Hyperventilation
____ A crawling sensation under the skin
____ A tight band around the head
____ Disorientation or unreal feelings
____ Eyes playing strange tricks
____ Overall muscle weakness
____ Sleeplessness
____ Nausea
____ Diarrhea
____ Frequent urination
____ Depression ⚠

If someone you love is exhibiting symptoms of a prolonged panicky or phobic state, get help immediately. Do not pass Go. Forget the two hundred dollars. Drop what you are doing, go straight to the wisest person you know (preferably someone with connections not only to the Big Guy but also to the medical and/or psychiatric community), and tell that person what you suspect. If your panic-stricken loved one can't (or won't) get help for him- or herself, at least get help for *yourself*. It can make a world of difference.

Anxiety is not a thing to take lightly. If you are that panic-traumatized person, start with your family doctor. Please understand that panic disorder (and its many variations) is *curable*. It might take meds, and it will, for sure, take effort and time. But it's curable. You don't have to live like this. Remember the words of King David in 1 Chronicles 28:20: "Be strong and courageous, and do the work. Do not be afraid or discouraged, for the LORD God . . . is with you."

He really is.

TAKE YOUR MEDS

Memorize this parting Scripture, Romans 15:13, from *The Message*:

"*Oh! May the God of green hope fill you up with joy, fill you up with peace, so that your believing lives, filled with the life-giving energy of the Holy Spirit, will brim over with hope!*"

RESOURCES

I had a stick of CareFree gum, but it didn't work. I felt pretty good while I was blowing that bubble, but as soon as the gum lost its flavor, I was back to pondering my mortality.

—MITCH HEDBERG

The following are just a few resources you might benefit from. Explore, but please don't take offense. Remember, they helped me. They may or may not flip your pancake. If they don't, find what does. Stretch that risk muscle.

HOW TO BEAT FEAR

Anxiety, Phobias, and Panic: A Step-by-Step Program for Regaining Control of Your Life by Reneau Z. Peurifoy (Warner, 2005). This is a great resource.

Feel the Fear and Do It Anyway by Dr. Susan Jeffers (Random House, 2007). Terrific book!

How to Stop Worrying and Start Living: Time-Tested Methods for Conquering Worry by Dale Carnegie (Simon & Schuster, 1984). A classic Carnegie book full of inspiration, stories, and tips.

Lies Women Believe and the Truth That Sets Them Free by Nancy Leigh DeMoss (Moody Press, 2002). A good read with a lot of godly wisdom.

Living Fear Free: Overcoming Agoraphobia—The Anxiety/Panic Syndrome by Melvin Green (Warner Books, 1989). Loaded with good information about panic disorder.

Telling Yourself the Truth: Find Your Way Out of Depression, Anxiety, Fear, Anger, and Other Common Problems by Applying the Principles of Misbelief Therapy by William Backus and Marie Chapian (Bethany House, 2000). This was where I first read about agoraphobia. It has some wonderful ways to help take action against the lies we believe. Good for dealing with many negative behaviors and thought processes. Much godly wisdom.

You Can't Afford the Luxury of a Negative Thought by Peter McWilliams (Prelude Press, 1995). Any of the Life 101 series of books is great fun and really inspirational. Not written from a Christian perspective, so keep that in mind.

PERSONAL AND SPIRITUAL GROWTH

The Mitford series by Jan Karon (boxed set by Penguin, 2002). You can't help but be changed by a trip to this delightful South Carolina town.

Hinds' Feet On High Places by Hannah Hurnard (Kingsway Publications, 2001). Great story for people who struggle. (Oops, I guess that's all of us!)

The Language of Love: How to Quickly Communicate Your Feelings and Needs by Dr. Gary Smalley and Dr. John Trent (Focus on the Family Publishing, 1999). Powerful! I use what I learned from this book—All! The! Time!

Lifetime Guarantee: Making Your Christian Life Work and What to Do When It Doesn't by Dr. Bill Gillham (Harvest House Publishers, 1993). I really appreciate Dr. Gillham's take on so much of the Christian walk.

The Problem of Pain by C. S. Lewis (Touchstone, 1996). A great book to begin exploring this brilliant thinker. If your only experience with Lewis is the Narnia series (a fabulous series), it's time to discover his other works. Start here.

What's So Amazing About Grace? by Philip Yancey (Zondervan, 1997). Yancey is another brilliant thinker. This is his best work.

GETTING TO KNOW GOD

The Attributes of God: A Journey into the Father's Heart by A. W. Tozer (Christian Publications, 1998). Cerebral, but worth the effort.

Believing God: Experiencing a Fresh Explosion of Faith by Beth Moore (LifeWay, 2005). DO THIS! It's great!

The Day I Was Crucified: As Told by Jesus Christ by Gene Edwards (Deeper Life Publishers, 2004). Edwards is a strange little writer, but WOW! It's like another layer of the movie *The Passion of the Christ*.

Loving God Up Close: Rekindling Your Relationship with the Holy Spirit by Calvin Miller (Warner Faith Books, 2004). Excellent.

No Wonder They Call Him the Savior: Experiencing the Truth of the Cross by Max Lucado (Thomas Nelson, 2005). If you've never tried Lucado . . . well, you should. This is one of his early works, but they're all absolutely incredible.

The Singer (part of a trilogy) by Calvin Miller (InterVarsity, 2001). A weird, wonderful, poetic allegory. You can read it in an hour or so, but it'll never leave you.

Who Moved the Stone? by Frank Morison (Authentic Media, 2006). An unbelieving criminologist looks at the evidence for Christ's resurrection. Excellent for your own faith.

OTHER RESOURCES FOR FURTHER HEALING

Boundaries: When to Say Yes, When to Say No, to Take Control of Your Life by Dr. Henry Cloud and Dr. John Townsend (Running Press, 2004). Helps to give perspective on what is yours and what isn't as you aim toward health.

Unlocking the Secrets of Your Childhood Memories by Kevin Leman and Randy Carlson (Thomas Nelson, 2001). Great resource to help heal painful memories.

Prescription for Nutritional Healing by Phyllis Balch (some editions also by James Balch; Avery, 2006). A great resource for ideas for alternative treatments, without downplaying traditional medicines. I go to this before I check any other source because I like its whole-body approach.

GOING TO ARUBA

I prefer humor books when I need some down time, but feel free to find what tickles your funny bone or lifts your spirits.

A Walk in the Woods by Bill Bryson (Black Swan, 1998). Bryson is such a great writer—very witty—you even forget you're learning something. He doesn't write from a Christian perspective, in case that bothers you.

Dave Barry's Book of Bad Songs by Dave Barry (Andrews McMeel Publishing, 2000). Anything Dave Barry does is absolutely silly. Some people like it, some don't. If you've never tried any of his humor (be warned, it's *very* silly!), start here.

Last Trout in Venice: The Far-Flung Escapades of an Accidental Adventurer by Doug Lansky (Travelers' Tales, 2001). I've just discovered him. Interesting and fun so far. He's not writing from a Christian perspective, FYI.

The Fun Factor: Unleashing the Power of Humor at Home and on the Job by Clifford Kuhn (Minerva Books, 2003). A practical "textbook" on how to implement humor.

Uncle John's Slightly Irregular Bathroom Reader by the Bathroom Readers' Institute (Portable Press, 2004). This isn't a funny book, but it is an excellent diversion. I even took one (there are at least seventeen in the series) with me to the hospital when I was ready to deliver Meghan. Lots of interesting stories, long and short. Keeps your mind occupied without becoming overwhelmed.

PERSONALITY

Please Understand Me: Character & Temperament Types by David Keirsey and Marilyn Bates (Prometheus Nemesis Book

Company, 1984). A terrific book for regular people about the Myers-Briggs [Personality] Type Indicator. Has a self-grading quiz and detailed breakdown for each type.

The Two Sides of Love by Dr. Gary Smalley and Dr. John Trent (Tyndale House, 2006). This is a great resource to begin understanding personalities from a Christian perspective. The authors use the otter, lion, beaver, and golden retriever as their type indicators, so the process is fun and revealing. Probably one of my favorites, especially for anyone starting out in this area.

For more information visit:
www.marcybryan.com
and
www.scaredsilly.blogspot.com

NOTES

Quotations that were not noted were taken from among the following Web sites: www.thinkexist.com, www.brainyquote.com, www.worldofquotes.com, www.wikiquote.org, www.workinghumor. com, www.dogquotations.com, www.findquotations.com, www. quoteland.com, and www.imdb.com.

INTRODUCTION

1. P. J. O'Rourke. Quoted in *The Oxford Dictionary of Humorous Quotations*, edited by Ned Sherrin (Oxford, NY: Oxford University Press, 1996), 335.

CHAPTER 1

1. www.flmnh.ufl.edu/fish/sharks/statistics/beachattacks.htm (accessed August 9, 2006).

2. www.algy.com/anxiety.

3. Susan Jeffers, *Feel the Fear and Do It Anyway* (New York: Random House, 1987), 13–15.

4. Bureau of Transportation Statistics, www.bts.gov/press_ releases/2006/bts020_06/html (accessed August 9, 2006).

5. National Transportation Safety Board, www.ntsb.gov/ pressrel/2006/060317.htm (accessed August 9, 2006).

6. Ron Nielsen and Fearless-Flight.com, www.fearless-flight.com/ flight-safety/statistics.php (accessed August 9, 2006).

7. James F. Balch and Phyllis A. Balch, *Prescription for Nutritional Healing*, second edition (Garden City Park, New York: Avery Publishing Group, 1997), 131–132.

CHAPTER 2

1. www.dictionary.reference.com.

2. Information in this section was taken from Holmes-Rahe Stress Test, "The Social Readjustment Rating Scale," *Journal of Psychosomatic Research* (1967), 213–218, as seen on www.unl.edu/ECSE/960/strestst.html (accessed August 9, 2006).

3. Clayton Tucker-Ladd and the Self-Help Foundation, www.psychologicalselfhelp.org/Chapter6/chap6_49.html (and _50.html) (accessed August 9, 2006).

4. Reneau Z. Peurifoy, *Anxiety, Phobias and Panic: Taking Charge and Conquering Fear,* second edition (n.p.: LifeSkills, 1988, 1992), 118.

5. C. S. Lewis, *Letters to an American Lady* © 1967 Wm B. Eerdmans Publishing Company, Grand Rapids, Michigan. Reprinted by permission of the publisher. All rights reserved. (Quoted here from an edition published by Pyramid Publications for Eerdmans, 1971, reprinted 1998, 110.)

6. See how they describe it. Gary Smalley and John Trent, *The Language of Love: How to Quickly Communicate Your Feelings and Needs* (Pomona, CA: Focus on the Family Publishing, 1999), chapters 5–6.

CHAPTER 3

1. I've adapted the material in this section (obviously!) from an article I have on file: "Memories of Fear: How the Brain Stores and Retrieves Physiologic States, Feelings, Behavior and Thoughts from Traumatic Events" by Bruce D. Perry.

2. Noted by Doug Turner, "Flourishing with the Positive," *Positive Psychology News Daily, NY,* February 15, 2007, http://pos-psych.com/news/doug-turner/20070215106 (accessed May 11, 2007).

3. "Anxious Famous People," www.algy.com/anxiety/famous.php (accessed August 10, 2006).

4. American Academy of Pediatrics, "Television and the Family," www.aap.org/family/tv1.htm.

5. Mary Anne Layden. Quoted by Ryan Singel, "Internet Porn: Worse Than Crack?" November 19, 2004, www.wired.com/news/technology/w,65772-0.html (accessed August 10, 2006).

CHAPTER 4

1. Ken Ownby, e-mail message to author, April 18, 2006.

2. www.cnnmoney.printthis.clickability.com/ pt.cpt?action=cpt&title and www. Pageuser.auctions.yahoo.com/ auction/89133085?aucview=0x70 (accessed August 10, 2006).

3. Viktor E. Frankl, *Man's Search for Meaning* (New York: Simon & Schuster, 1984), 75.

CHAPTER 5

1. www.reformed.org/documents/WSC_frames.html.

2. U. S. Department of Justice, "Criminal Sentencing Statistics," www.ojp.usdoj.gov/bjs/sent.htm (accessed August 10, 2006).

3. Bathroom Readers' Institute, *Uncle John's Colossal Collection of Quotable Quotes* (Ashland, Oregon: Portable Press, 2004), 113.

4. *Mere Christianity* by C. S. Lewis copyright © C. S. Lewis Pte. Ltd. 1942, 1943, 1944, 1952. (Quoted here from an edition published New York: MacMillan Publishing, 1979, 36.)

CHAPTER 6

1. Read the book yourself. The edition I have is Henry Cloud and John Townsend, *Boundaries: When to Say Yes, When to Say No, to Take Control of Your Life* (Grand Rapids: Zondervan, 1992).

2. Based on Bill Gillham, *Lifetime Guarantee* (Eugene, Oregon: Harvest House Publishers, 1993), 164–171.

CHAPTER 7

1. Quoted in Philip Yancey, *What's So Amazing About Grace?* (Grand Rapids, Michigan: Zondervan Publishing House, 1997), 71.

2. Brennan Manning. Quoted by James Bryan Smith, *Rich Mullins: An Arrow Pointing to Heaven* (Nashville, Tennessee: Broadman & Holman Publishers, 2000), 60.

CHAPTER 8

1. I guess we'll never know who wrote the fortune cookie message noted by Robert Byrne, *The 2,548 Best Things Anybody Ever Said* (New York: BBS Publishing Corporation, 1996), book section III, #414.

2. Mickey Friedman. Quoted by Robert Byrne, *The 2,548 Best Things Anybody Ever Said* (New York: BBS Publishing Corporation, 1996), book section III, #302.

CHAPTER 9

1. I heard Paula Deen at a Louisville, Kentucky, public library on April 20, 2007.

2. *The Revell Bible Dictionary* (Grand Rapids, Michigan: Fleming H. Revell Company [Baker], 1994), 686.

3. http://www.blueletterbible.org/cgi-bin/words.pl?book=1Ti&chapter=4&verse=15&strongs=3191&page (accessed April 13, 2007).

CHAPTER 10

1. Ann Landers. Quoted by Bathroom Readers' Institute, *Uncle John's Colossal Collection of Quotable Quotes* (Ashland, Oregon: Portable Press, 2004), 207.

2. *The Problem of Pain* by C. S. Lewis copyright © C. S. Lewis Pte. Ltd. 1940. Extract reprinted by permission. (Quoted here from an edition published New York: Simon & Schuster, 1996, 103.)

EPILOGUE

1. Quoted by Peter McWilliams, *The LIFE 101 Quote Book* (Los Angeles, CA: Prelude Press, 1996), 306.

2. This list adapted from Melvin Green, *Living Fear Free: Overcoming Agoraphobia—The Anxiety/Panic Syndrome* (New York: Warner Books, 1987), 19.

If you liked *Scared Silly*, we think you'll like these books!

For more information visit
www.standardpub.com
or call 1-800-543-1301.